Praise for *Starter Dog*

"Among the many canine classics I've read, *Starter Dog* is the leader of the pack. It's a beautiful tribute to a long marriage in which kindness toward a dog unlocks stored affection between spouses. It is also a powerful meditation on the pleasures of a life spent discovering the world from a dog's perspective instead of slogging at the office. With humor and insight, Rona proves that some things about being human are best learned from a dog. I loved this book."

—Catherine Gildiner, *New York Times* bestselling author of *Good Morning, Monster*

"A delightful romp with a mutt for all hearts."

—Donna Morrissey, bestselling author of *Pluck*

"An elegant and engaging tale. With this tender invitation to get to know her beloved pup Casey, Rona Maynard makes dog lovers of us all—even the most ardent of cat people like me!"

—Mark Henick, mental health advocate and bestselling author of *So-Called Normal*

"A wise woman's reassessment of life and love, *Starter Dog* is a beautifully felt, thoughtful and often funny read. While the rescue mutt may be billed as the star of the show, Maynard herself commands center stage, evolving in surprising ways. Unfailingly observant, this book is deeply life-affirming—a joy to read."

—Ann Dowsett Johnston, bestselling author of *Drink: The Intimate Relationship Between Women and Alcohol*

T0130771

"As a late convert to the world of dogs myself, I devoured Rona Maynard's gorgeous, engaging prose as fast as my pup wolfs down her morning kibble. *Starter Dog* is far more than a tale of a woman and her dog. This gem of a book showed me it's still possible to find simple, everyday beauty in an uncertain world and that love and connection, discovered one daily walk at a time, beat ambition and accomplishment. I loved the heart and wisdom woven through this inspirational book, and—dog lover or not—you'll love it too."

—Laura Davis, author of *The Burning Light of Two Stars* and *The Courage to Heal*

"When you buy yourself a copy of this funny, honest adventure of a book (and you must), you're going to want to clear a few hours and read every word. God, Rona Maynard is a good writer."

—Abigail Thomas, *New York Times* bestselling author of *A Three Dog Life* and *Still Life at Eighty*

"*Starter Dog* is an enchanting love story between a pet and his human. Rona Maynard shows us with marvelous wit and sensitivity how the world is expanded and enhanced by the companionship of a dog."

—Hilma Wolitzer, author of *Today a Woman Went Mad in the Supermarket: Stories*

STARTER DOG

My Path to Joy, Belonging and Loving This World

Rona Maynard

Published by ECW Press
665 Gerrard Street East
Toronto, Ontario, Canada M4M 1Y2
416-694-3348 / info@ecwpress.com

Editor for the Press: Susan Renouf
Copy editor: Jennifer Knoch
Front cover photograph: Heather Pollock
Back cover photograph: Peter Bregg

LIBRARY AND ARCHIVES CANADA CATALOGUING
IN PUBLICATION

Title: Starter dog : my path to joy, belonging and loving
this world / Rona Maynard.

Names: Maynard, Rona, author.

Identifiers: Canadiana (print) 20220483108 | Canadiana
(ebook) 20220483248

ISBN 978-1-77041-723-6 (softcover)
ISBN 978-1-77852-156-0 (ePub)
ISBN 978-1-77852-157-7 (PDF)
ISBN 978-1-77852-158-4 (Kindle)

Subjects: LCSH: Maynard, Rona. | LCSH: Dogs—
Canada—Anecdotes. | LCSH: Dog owners—Canada—
Anecdotes. | LCSH: Human-animal relationships.

Classification: LCC SF426.2 .M39 2023
| DDC 636.7—dc23

This book is funded in part by the Government of Canada. *Ce livre est financé en partie par le gouvernement
du Canada.* We acknowledge the support of the Canada Council for the Arts. *Nous remercions le Conseil des
arts du Canada de son soutien.* We acknowledge the funding support of the Ontario Arts Council (OAC),
an agency of the Government of Ontario. We also acknowledge the support of the Government of Ontario
through the Ontario Book Publishing Tax Credit, and through Ontario Creates.

ONTARIO CREATES

ONTARIO ARTS COUNCIL
CONSEIL DES ARTS DE L'ONTARIO
an Ontario government agency
un organisme du gouvernement de l'Ontario

Canada Council
for the Arts

Conseil des arts
du Canada

Canadä

PRINTED AND BOUND IN CANADA   PRINTING: MARQUIS   5 4 3 2 1

MIX
Paper from
responsible sources
FSC® C103567

For my husband, who wanted a dog,
and in memory of my father,
for his tenderness toward all living creatures

Contents

Author's Note

You know what they say about dog books: "The dog always dies in the end." Not this book. You can relax.

When my senior dog leaps at squirrels like a puppy, I can almost believe he'll live forever. I'm a senior human, old enough to know better. Every story I tell, including this one, is to some degree about time and what it carries off—people I loved or used to be, animals who found the sunniest corners of places I called home. Every beginning holds the seed of an ending. But first there will be marvels, the great astonishment that sweeps away the same old, same old. First there will be fun. A year offers 525,600 minutes. You want more. It's only human. And yet a minute, fully lived, can feel like all the time in the world.

Let's take a walk with a very good boy. He can't wait to get started.

Part I: Joy

Yes, Let's

When my husband said, "Let's get a dog," I nearly retorted, "Let's not." I could think of three good reasons to veto this notion on the spot. But there sat Paul with his hand on mine and that dreamy yet resolute look I've learned not to take lightly. Waiting for me to say, "Yes, let's."

We had a pattern: He brought me an idea, I told him why it might not work.

Let's spend the winter in Florida: But what about my Pilates class in Toronto? What about the Saturday farmers' market?

Let's set the alarm for 3 a.m. and watch the meteor shower of a lifetime: But I might never get back to sleep.

Let's get married: But we've known each other five months. We're still in school. Can't we wait?

He's called me negative a time or two—a bit harsh, I think. Someone has to be on guard for the hidden flaws in a plan, the kernel of disappointment embedded in a hope. Besides, it's not as if I ever say no. Instead I wait to be jollied along, and eventually say, "Okay, if . . ." or "Could be interesting." Never "Yes, let's."

In more than 40 years of marriage, we'd managed fine without a dog. The time for a dog, if it ever existed, was back when we had a son at home to play fetch. Other couples we knew had buried their last dog and were hitting the road in an RV or training to hike the Camino, yet Paul seemed to think we should tie ourselves down. For God's sake, why? He felt like having a dog, that was why. He seemed to think that if I opened my mind, I'd feel the same way. And how forthright he'd been about this out-of-the-blue proposal. No "What if . . . ?" or "I've been thinking we could . . ." He was ready to look for a dog.

It had been another fine meal until this matter of the dog. Something seasonal cooked in extra-virgin olive oil, a complementary wine, around us artwork steeped in personal history. No decorator would have paired my father's sinuous paintings of the British Columbia coast with the prancing lizard carved from a single piece of wood, a souvenir of the Dominican Republic. We never knew the name of the Dominican carver, but his lizard and the Douglas firs looked equally at home in the eclectic domain we'd assembled piece by piece and had entirely to ourselves. When our last cat was alive, ginger fur collected in corners and clung to our pants. A dog would disarrange the order we'd finally achieved. "There'd be fur all over everything again. Remember when we had to brush ourselves down before we went anywhere?"

Those were the days of boardrooms and black-tie galas. I edited *Chatelaine*, a prominent women's magazine; Paul published news and business magazines for the same parent company. When the Queen came to Toronto, we were summoned to a dinner in her honor at the Royal York Hotel, along with some 700 other local worthies. Anywhere we went now, we could go with fur on our backsides. Paul said, "We'll get a non-shedding breed."

So much for disqualifying problem number one. Number two would be closer to his heart. "How are we supposed to travel? Could we have brought a dog to London or Paris? We'd have to leave the dog in a kennel. Think of the expense. The inconvenience."

"We'll work it out, take more road trips. Use your imagination."

One of us had to be practical. Dogs need to walk. A lot. Enter disqualifying problem number three. Paul's knees had recently been so bad that he couldn't walk two blocks to the bank without pausing on a bench to rest. He no longer needed his cane but often spent the better part of a day at his desk, breaking only to make a tuna melt or throw in a load of laundry. An oldster's lifestyle, yet Paul was barely 63, too young to qualify for a senior's transit pass.

I could already hear myself asking, through gritted teeth, "Dear, when are you planning to walk the dog?" before eventually taking the dog out myself, seething with resentment. We'd been down that road as newlyweds arguing about who'd wash the scrambled-egg pan. Damned if I was going back to that for a dog.

I laid it on the line. "Are you sure you're up for all that walking?" Meaning "I'm sure you're not."

He was. After canvassing friends with dogs, he knew the walking regimens of Scooter, Murphy and Charlie. Any dog of ours would match them all. Absolutely, Paul would hold up his end. I wouldn't have to do a minute more than my share. One thing about my husband: He's a man of his word. "It'll be fun. You'll see."

Fun wasn't on my must-have list. I liked quiet, and we had plenty, pierced only by the whir of the espresso machine and the vibration of the fridge. The morning rustle of the *Globe and Mail* had gone silent when we switched to online news. And one day now unfolded much like any other, no calls from the school or crises at the office to disturb our peace. In fact, hardly anyone called us now except scammers and the dentist's office.

A neighbor's door slammed shut. Paul was still waiting for his answer. I couldn't bring myself to say yes to the dog, but no was out of the question. He'd forgive me; that wasn't the issue. *Rona will be Rona*, he'd think, as I had often thought *Paul will be Paul*. Whatever else we'd done and failed to do in more than 40 years of marriage, we both gave each other room to be ourselves. I chose a man who loved dogs. Always had, always would. Whenever I thought of Paul's tender side, a dog came to mind soon enough. That night with his hand on mine, I saw quite a few dogs, though none had been ours. They took me back through every phase of our marriage.

Here we are at the airport in the executive years, bound for who-knows-what European capital. Paul, being Paul, has left the office at the last conceivable moment and packed while the limo waited at our door. Checking in for an overseas flight somewhat later than I had hoped, we hear whimpering at our feet. A German shepherd, alone in a crate that rocks with his misery. We're about to drink champagne in business class while the dog shivers in the hold. Paul kneels to comfort him and lingers there, trying the patience of the check-in clerk. "I'll have to ask you to move along, sir. This guy needs to settle down and you're not helping." I can bear the German shepherd's anxiety, but I ache for my husband.

I scroll further back to our striving years in the magazine industry. I'm rewriting copy at a fashion magazine as green as I am (until recently a teen magazine); Paul has just left a business lunch when he passes a pet shop and finds himself smitten by a furiously wagging puppy who might as well be calling to him alone, "Hey, you! What about me?" Paul thinks about the puppy all the way to his office, where the first thing he does is reach for the phone. I can't believe this cockamamie talk about a puppy. Such a lively little fellow, according to Paul. Our son would love him. A kid should have a dog, right?

I won't hear another word about the puppy. "Ben already has a cat. He's too young to look after a dog, and we're much too busy. By the way, was that a liquid lunch?"

Dogs in elevators, dogs at traffic lights. Dogs in San Francisco, Amsterdam and Buenos Aires. I never noticed them until Paul began to say, as much to himself as to the people walking them, "I love dogs." All of them stand-ins for the only dog he ever had. He told me the story on our first date, at a long-vanished coffee shop near the campus.

His father had always hated dogs but was persuaded by Paul and his sisters to let one join the family. Her name was Brandy, and she didn't last long. On the brink of a move, she vanished. Gone to a farm, the parental story went. Paul quietly concluded that his parents were lying. His father wanted to be rid of Brandy, and moving provided an excuse. Paul and the dog were just getting started when she was carried off to an uncertain fate.

I'd come to the coffee shop in a what-the-hell frame of mind. Paul struck me as caustic and full of himself—too sharp-witted to brush off, but not boyfriend material. Brandy revealed another Paul. She might as well have been under the chrome table, pawing my leg as dogs do when your attention is required. More than 40 years after our first date, she was at it again.

A dog at our stage? Maybe not such a wild idea. Paul's other let's-do-it proposals had worked out surprisingly well. Take winter in Florida, a wild idea to no one in Toronto but me. I didn't miss Pilates while strolling along Tampa Bay on a February morning, dewy grass brushing my bare ankles. And the Leonid meteor shower, backdropped by the cloudless sky above a hiking spa in Utah, was pure magic. I spun, giddy with amazement as shooting stars filled the sky while around me goal-conscious grownups, who earlier that day had been checking the calorie count on the high-fiber cereal, shrieked like children at a fairground. I might have missed it all for another hour of sleep.

As for getting married at 21, in a ragtag city hall ceremony, how could anyone call it a mistake? We'd witnessed the crash-and-burn divorces of couples who were happy once, or seemed to be. Happier than we were, I'd have said in our early years. Those couples had the sense not to marry until they could afford a marriage bed. They had proper wedding china, not bits of this and that from Honest Ed's. But we were the ones still sitting down to dinner at the table with the scarred leaf, pacing ourselves to make the wine last while conversation ranged far and wide—only to land on "Let's get a dog."

Had Paul ever sold me on a bad idea? Looking back, I came up with one: painting the study door purple. This dog was almost certainly another stroke of inspiration. Then again, it might be another purple door. White paint took care of the wrong color. The wrong dog would mean a guilt-ridden trip to the Humane Society. And I doubted any dog could be right for me.

Beside our dining room table hangs a portrait of me, a birthday gift from Paul. My gaze drifted there while I thought about the dog. An artist friend, Gerda Neubacher, had caught me in a rare moment of abandon. Newly sprung from *Chatelaine*, I'm twirling with hope for the memoir I've just started after years spent polishing other people's prose. Gerda has lent me her biggest straw hat and tied around it a chiffon scarf that floats on the early-summer breeze like the tail of a kite. I'd never have thought of wearing anything so flamboyant as that scarf.

That day on Gerda's roof deck, I didn't think this portrait would ever hang on my wall. She was working on a series of portraits and invited me to take part. There was no expectation I would buy mine; wall space was tight in our condo. But Paul was so taken with the portrait that he bought it for my birthday, trusting that we'd find a space. Every time I glanced at Gerda's painting, I wanted to be that levitating woman, who's on the brink of something and open to whatever it might be. I looked again at the painted me and considered the dog my husband believed we should have. The time had come for the only kind of yes I could muster. "Okay, then. I'm in. But there's one condition. The dog stays out of our bed. I'm not having paw prints on our sheets."

We had a deal. Like my husband, I keep my word. I might badger, guilt-trip or wheedle, but I cannot break a promise. A cheerful presence at our feet didn't sound so bad, especially if it got Paul moving again. Since I couldn't figure out what I wanted for myself, I might as well get behind what my husband wanted. Let his wanting lift me like a trailing scarf on a breeze. I could learn to like a dog well enough. Love was too big a stretch, not that it mattered. I had plenty of love already.

Something was missing from my life, and it sure as hell wasn't a dog. Once upon a time I had felt connected to a project greater than myself. I went out every morning to a place in the world where I belonged, and came home refreshed by its ever-changing buzz and hum. The difference I made there was never mine alone; I had a team. A job was my bridge to that place, that belonging. I walked away convinced another bridge would appear. Not a job, I was done with all that, but some other route to the world. I told anyone who asked about my plans, "I'm going to surprise myself."

Eight years later, I still hadn't. Might as well admit it: Surprises were not my thing. I would look at my portrait with a sinking heart. Where was that dancing woman? Had she ever been real?

I'd been casting about for a Project. Lots of moving parts, a mission that engaged me, a sidekick or two whose gifts would complement mine. I longed for the Project the way, in my teens, I had longed to fall in love, with a hunger for completion that beat against my ribcage. "Any day he'll appear" had become "Any day inspiration will strike," but time was running out to pull this Project into focus.

A poem by Mary Oliver, "When Death Comes," kept calling me. With more years behind me than ahead, I too had been thinking of death as a hungry bear closing in. Yet the poet knew something I didn't. She had turned her attention from dying to full-tilt living. She wanted to leave this world as a passionate and satisfied lover of all its delights, not as a mere visitor. That sounded good to me. But unlike Mary Oliver, I wasn't married to amazement. I couldn't imagine how it felt to take the world in my arms. So far, perhaps forever, I was just passing through.

The way things were going, I might never find the Project. Instead I'd be looking for a dog I didn't want. Love makes you do the damnedest things.

The One

Paul knew from the get-go what kind of dog we should have. "A friendly dog. A smart dog. A *doggy* dog." Dogginess, as I understood it, meant trash-eating, crotch-sniffing, mud-rolling disregard for human ways. A doggy dog would defend his people, but should never have his dignity undone by a topknot in his curls or an Ewok costume for Halloween. He'd be a knocked-around mutt, light on credentials but long on character. In short, a rescue dog. With thousands of dogs euthanized every year, Paul thought we might as well do the responsible thing.

A rescue dog might do for Paul, but not for me. I had to know what *kind* of dog we were getting—the temperament, the health profile. As I understood it, that meant a breed, to be determined by research. Friends with dogs couldn't wait to help me out. They bombarded me with pitches for their own breed of choice, from the perky and portable Boston terrier (so affectionate!) to the hundred-pound-plus Newfoundland (so gentle!). Depending on who had just bent my ear, I'd tell Paul we couldn't do better than a winsome goldendoodle or a grandchild-friendly Cavalier King Charles spaniel.

I took to buttonholing strangers with appealing dogs (of course the One would be a dog people stop to admire). The day I met my first Havanese, I suggested to Paul that we should have one too. Easy to train, the perfect size for condo living, a tireless playmate for our six-year-old grandson. How could we go wrong? Malcolm Gladwell had a Havanese, the inspiration for a piece in the *New Yorker*. By that logic, I might have fantasized about a Mexican hairless dog like the ones Frida Kahlo used to fondle, but logic didn't figure in my ruminations. I fired off an email to a well-respected breeder of Havanese whose reply could have filled a few magazine pages. Yes, his pups were "all delicious" and incredibly loving. In fact, "They do not enjoy being alone . . . It would make them nuts to be closed off in another room . . . " Perish the thought. It makes me nuts to have someone forever at my side, even if that someone is a dog. No Havanese for us.

Until I recognized the One, we wouldn't have a dog. I never set out to kill the plan. All I had to do was indulge my lifelong habit of holding out for an ideal. All my husband had to do was let it happen.

I was forming an image of the One. Snub nose, button eyes, fur you could run your hands through, like the dog in a Little Golden Book I loved at three and still keep close at hand—*The Sailor Dog*, one of Margaret Wise Brown's more obscure collaborations with the children's illustrator Garth Williams (of *Stuart Little*, *Charlotte's Web* and the Little House series). Unlike any dog who ever lived,

Scuppers is a solitary soul who will not be deterred from his dream of going to sea, all by himself. Garth Williams's illustrations endeared Scuppers to me as a surrogate self with the features of a terrier and the emotions of a human child not about to be bossed around by grownups. By day he surveys the horizon from the bridge of his ship, tail wagging through the slit in his shiny yellow raincoat. At night he curls up in his bunk, looking just like a dog, if a dog had special hooks for his hat, his rope, his pants and his spyglass.

Only a person with no appreciation for dogs would be drawn to a canine loner with a hankering for order. Paul had grown accustomed to my quoting breed profiles from DogTime.com, but I was not about to say, while brandishing *The Sailor Dog*, "How about a dog like Scuppers?"

I came around to the idea of a rescue dog. Maybe we could rescue a dog like Scuppers. No waiting in line with a breeder, no housebreaking a puppy in an eighth-floor condo. How hard could it be to rescue the One, with all those dogs waiting for homes?

A whole lot harder than I thought. We had to rule out the fireballs who needed a yard to romp in, the traumatized dogs with short fuses and mysterious phobias, the palliative care dogs waiting for a gentle exit from this world. Likely-looking dogs—with or without a snub nose and button eyes—were snapped up within days, and we always had somewhere to go before making our move. "Let's get serious after Berlin," one of us would say. But after Berlin came New York or Florida, with not enough time in between for the three-month bonding period we planned to give the One. Why wait all those years for a dog if we were going to cut corners?

A year of fitful searching went by, then two. We bought an SUV with plenty of room for a dog. Rented a dog-friendly bungalow for our next winter in St. Petersburg, with a broad veranda where our mutt could snooze under a ceiling fan. Checked in dogless, with plans to bring the One next year. People started to ask, "Are you still talking about a dog?" with "talking" in audible italics. Our son, Ben, had promised to dog-sit. Now he rolled his eyes when we mentioned the dog.

At this rate the One would go the way of the second child we never got around to having, the getaway place in Florida we didn't buy when the market was on our side and a particularly glorious urban hike I never took with my friend Val, who was stricken with a lethal brain tumor while I thought we could take our sweet time. We'd already walked the route once, a ramble through one of Toronto's lush ravines. For each of us, it was a subway ride away. But one of us was always traveling, moving or working all weekend. Someday the time would be right.

I'd come to think of the slide from "someday" to "never" as an inescapable part of growing older, like struggling to hear in crowded restaurants. Imperceptibly, I'd become that diner who's forever asking tablemates, too loudly, "What's that you said?" Only *that* wasn't just a snippet of a story, but entire life chapters postponed for "someday" and lost in a blur of might-have-beens.

I'd never get to live those lost chapters, but I could do the next-best thing: yank the prospect of a dog from the cliff of someday while time allowed. Diana Athill, whose plainspoken memoir on aging I dip into a few times a year, was not given to regrets but wrote at 89 that she'd grown too old to walk the pug puppy she had always wanted. I underlined the passage as a warning to myself.

Paul is certain he's the one who finally said, "Enough foot-dragging! Time to get this dog!" I'm equally certain it was me. Although I still had mixed feelings about the dog, I dreaded becoming a gutless fogey. We cancelled a trip to South Africa and dove back into the dog rescue sites. On separate computers, we scrolled past dozens of dogs, all impossible for various reasons.

We got our hopes up for a beagle—middle-aged but still perky—who was already taken. Then Tucker showed up on Paul's screen, mouth wide open as if in expectation of a treat. "What a handsome boy!" the caption burbled (to be described in any other terms, he'd have to be missing an eye and most of his fur). Lab-pug mix, the listing said. Who knew such a creature existed? He looked nothing like Scuppers, but I was in no mood to quibble. Best of a bad lot, I figured. Paul clicked "Ask about me." As it turned out, the rescue people did the asking.

We filled out a form that tested our mettle. (Would anything prompt us to give up a dog? All we could think of was chewing the furniture.) We drummed up references from friends with dogs. We waited. "Still no word on Tucker," Paul would say. Tucker must have already found a home. At that very moment he'd be rolling on the floor with someone's kids or chasing a Frisbee in a fenced yard. Perhaps it was better that way. Tucker was a young dog, and young dogs need to blow off steam. We weren't exactly young humans.

As we braced ourselves for another dispiriting tour of the adoption sites, we finally heard from the rescue people. Yes, Tucker was still on offer. We were first in line, with all the paperwork in order. Some rescue organizations require a home visit, some grill adopters on their habits and schedules. A few decline all inquiries from those without a fenced yard. Not this one. A routine look-see, and we were good to go.

I shared the news with a woman at my gym as we toweled ourselves down, side by side, faces still flushed from the shower. Jeanette always spoke of her two dogs the way some people speak of their children. I felt certain she would say, "Best move you'll ever make," but her eyes went steely. Last time I'd seen that look, I was a junior editor being dressed down for letting the issue go to press with "Turn to page 00" where the page number should have been. "You do realize, Rona," Jeanette began (anyone who says, "You do realize" has pretty much decided you don't), "this is a ten-year commitment." I saw what she was thinking: Paul and I might not stay the course. I knew better. If we were the quitting kind, we'd have quit on each other long ago.

Lucky Dog

The first time we saw the ginger mutt then known as Tucker, and before that as Shotgun, he was lurking at the feet of a ponytailed yenta named Liz, who called herself his foster mom. After standing in her doorway for what seemed like forever, we could have used a seat, but it wasn't on offer. She was too busy pitching the "perfect" starter dog for a couple of beginners in their 60s. Lovebug on the TV couch, new best friend for our grandson, condo-size at 30 pounds. Liz didn't see many like Tucker, so we'd be wise to snap him up. "The sad cases are the ones that stick around. Like Jessie here." I hadn't noticed Jessie, who cowered on the stairs and should have been a ball of fluff, but her fur had gone lank and patchy from neglect. "Owner was a hoarder, too old and sick to care for her dogs. Had quite a pack of 'em. Poor, terrified baby, she's been with me for weeks now."

Tucker, though, was one lucky dog, a survivor. Did we know about prisons where convicts train dogs for adoption? The convicts learn job skills and build self-esteem; the dogs learn how to get along in a family. We were looking at a graduate of one such program at a men's prison in Ohio. Tucker spent some of his puppyhood behind bars; then, we were told, he waited in a high-kill shelter for someone to take him home. As time ran out, he was spirited away to Toronto by a band of volunteers who have made it their mission to save dogs from death. He landed at Liz's suburban house—freshly neutered, just over one year old, all ready for his forever home (spelled "furever" on some of the rescue sites). "He's perfect for you," Liz repeated.

The dog didn't look so perfect to me. I noted the torn right ear, the bowlegs a bit spindly for the barrel chest, the woebegone air conveyed by his long snout. When he parked his rump on my foot, I gave him top marks for chutzpah. "See?" crowed Liz. "He likes you!" I saw where this was going. In her mind, I was already "Mom," a term that makes me cringe when the "child" isn't human.

I'd have shuffled my feet, but Tucker pinned me to the spot. His warmth penetrated my leather boot, encircling the arthritic big toe that hasn't bent since Brad Pitt married Jennifer Aniston. I rather liked having my bad toe swaddled by a dog but wasn't sure about the beast himself. Neither big nor little, dark nor light, he seemed as nondescript as a creature could be. I thought our starter dog should be exceptional. After all the years we'd spent without a dog, why settle for less? Tucker had a great story, I'd grant him that. Prison made him faintly exotic. Plenty of my friends had dogs, but none of theirs had been trained by a convict. Still, Tucker wasn't the dog I'd been expecting.

Paul gave me a let's-take-him look while playing it cool for Liz. "One last question," he began (the answer clearly wouldn't change a thing). "Does Tucker shed?"

"Oh, hardly at all!" Liz winked at Tucker, who had lost interest in my foot and was sniffing the floor tiles with rapt concentration. Any dog person would have known he was hunting for crumbs to lick.

What I knew about shedding had me spooked. Were we talking the occasional ginger hair on a cushion, or a permanent layer of ginger fur on everything black? "He's a dignified dog," Liz continued, back in yenta mode. Damn, she was good. Dignity counts for a lot with me, as she could probably tell from the cut of my hat, but I didn't see it in this jailbird mutt. On second thought, maybe I did. Tucker wasn't sniffing anymore. He stood his ground in Liz's hall as if he knew we were deciding his fate. Paws firmly planted, eyes fixed on Paul and me in supremely patient expectation.

If we were checking out a car in the showroom, this would be the moment for the test-drive. Dangling keys, the smell of new leather. Liz had a leash in her hand. "Why don't you two take this guy for a stroll, see for yourselves what a sweetie he is?"

Neither of us had ever walked a dog. The ones we knew as children romped out the door and all over the block to leave steaming mementos for the neighbors. Liz had to show us how to loop the leash around our palms and slip the poop bag on like an inside-out glove. But when it came to walking, we were on our own.

It was a raw, gray morning, just over a week before Easter. Not one car on Liz's suburban crescent, nobody but a solemn little girl on a bike with training wheels to see Paul and Tucker lurch all over the road. She stopped pedaling, mesmerized at the spectacle of an adult of grandparental years being bested by a ragamuffin dog. Round and round Tucker went, all furious confusion, chest muscles straining and snout to the ground in a canine version of competitive truck-pulling posture. "I have to hand it to Tucker," said Paul. "He's powerful for 30 pounds." Was that a flush of pride on my husband's face? He lifted heavy weights. I didn't. How would I manage this bruiser? The One was supposed to be at most 25 pounds, but I'd relented to expand our options.

As if we had any options. Of all the rescue dogs currently on offer, this dog was the only one not too big, too small, too old, too decrepit, too traumatized or too ugly (I didn't have a big enough heart for the homely dog nobody wants). Liz had a point; we'd better not drag our feet. In two years of desultory searching, we hadn't found a more suitable dog than the one dragging Paul in circles. If we went home to think it over, we'd be out of luck.

Tucker. That name would never cut it. Too trendy (number ten on Rover.com's list of most popular names for male dogs). And as I told Paul, it suggested unfortunate rhymes. "It's a name for a naughty limerick: There was a young rascal named Tucker . . . We've got to call him something else."

Paul looked amused. He saw what I'd just admitted: The ginger mutt was going to be ours. After all my what-ifs, not-yets and we-can-do-betters, I was about to sacrifice the order of my home and the predictable freedom of my days for this not-so-perfect dog who had just made a smiling fool of my husband.

Had it been up to Paul, we'd have taken our dog home the day we met, but he knew I needed more time. "My wife has a deadline to meet," he told Liz, pulling out his checkbook. "Okay with you if we come back for Tucker on Good Friday? We're not going to call him Tucker, by the way. We'd like to think about his name, so for now it would be best if you didn't call him anything."

Paul knew the truth about this deadline for a corporate white paper. I liked the people and the money, but the work didn't stir my heart. A gig substituting for the Project, the white paper absorbed disproportionate energy for polishing and fretting. It was still undergoing the 154th draft, only because hitting "send" would leave a void in my agenda. Poor nameless mutt, demoted to "Hey, you" for this.

He might as well have moved right in, for all the time I spent whipping the white paper into shape. Suddenly dog prep seemed more important. What a lot of stuff our dog would need. We bought him a shiny crimson leash ("I think red is his color," Paul said), a velveteen bed that matched the living room carpet, a stuffed raccoon that squeaked and a jumbo bag of Science Diet, the brand that sustained our last cat until age 17. We were contemplating small-batch treats (venison or pumpkin banana?) when the clerk said, "You'll be needing some of these. The bulk pack's a better deal." He held out a box of olive-green bags, its face bedecked with a cartoon dog fit for a toddler's pajamas. Oh, right. Those.

Our haul unpacked, I got busy dog-proofing the laundry room. What if the dog with no name got a sudden hankering for Windex? As I moved the plastic bags out of sniffing range, Paul said, "Dear, he's a dog, not a toddler. Don't you think he'd rather hunt for scraps in the kitchen garbage?"

"You wouldn't think it was so funny if we had to rush him to the vet to have a plastic bag removed from his gut piece by piece. It just happened to my friend Ellen's dog. It's incredible, the stuff some dogs eat. Nails, coins, cutlery, remotes, cell phone chargers. A Jack Russell terrier ate a ten-inch bread knife. You can see the X-ray online." When Paul showed no interest in the X-ray, I paused for another look at the white paper. This time I couldn't find anything to change. My inner faultfinder had shut up and left. The difference wasn't the few words I'd added or cut in revision number 154, which hardly differed from number 91, but the mental shift I'd made while getting ready for the One. That's what he'd become, by virtue of being good enough and available. I positioned his bed beside the dining room table so he could feel part of the conversation. Every time the One heard his name, he'd know where he belonged.

His name. The last item on our must-do list.

The Second Coming of Casey Jones

Paul and I had a fraught history with names. We named our son Ben, a reluctant compromise, after tearful arguments over the merits of Christopher, my pick, versus Paddington, Paul's idea of a joke but not funny to me. We eventually foisted Paddington on one of quite a few cats we strove to name with distinction. In those days we took our cue from T.S. Eliot in his whimsical mode: "The Naming of Cats is a difficult matter,/ It isn't just one of your holiday games." Our younger selves would have named a dog in the same spirit, had we ever resolved to adopt one. After much wearisome debate, we'd have paid homage to a Kurt Vonnegut character or a colorful and quotable minor player from the annals of baseball. In the countdown to Good Friday, adoption day, Paul suggested a simpler way to name Mr. Perfect—recycle the name of another dog close to our hearts. He might have mentioned Brandy, for the lost companion of his childhood, but I never knew Brandy. If we'd had other dogs, this would have been a snap. Neighbors of ours had raised a dynasty of dogs, all named Fred. Dorothy Parker named her dynasty of dogs Première, Deuxième and Troisième (Troy for short).

Paul suggested, "We could call him Nicky."

Nicky was the Maynard family's long-deceased poodle, as doggy a dog as ever flaunted his penis for company. His memory was a stone in my shoe. We couldn't have another Nicky.

A day or two passed before Paul tried again. "Let's call him Casey."

Casey, originally spelled K.C., was a name we'd spoken fondly every day for 17 years. It belonged to the ginger tabby Ben picked out as a child, along with his black-and-white littermate, Sam. We didn't plan on bringing two kittens home, just the liveliest of the bunch as determined by our test: Ben would dangle a foil ball from a string and take home the highest jumper. When two kittens jumped equally high, we couldn't leave one behind. Paul named them Sam and K.C. after Sam and K.C. Jones, two long-retired players for the Boston Celtics. I'd never heard of them and Ben was too young to care but the story took hold, and Paul's surname happens to be Jones. I had a hunch T.S. Eliot would approve. From day one we called our kittens Sam and K.C., never the other way around.

Sam died young, hit by a car in front of our house. K.C. was always Casey at the vet's, no matter how many times Paul told the origin story of his name. Without Sam, the story acquired a tinge of sadness. Our surviving cat became Casey Jones, like the engineer who in the words of Johnny Cash took "a trip to the promised land" when his passenger train ran into a stalled freight. Casey Jones the railwayman vaulted into the American songbook for slowing his train down in time to save the lives of his passengers. He's been celebrated by musical legends from Mississippi John Hurt to the Grateful Dead and beyond. Where are the songs about K.C. Jones the point guard?

The engineer's story left the basketball player's in the dust, although there was nothing heroic about the feline Casey Jones, who got the worst of every fight and had the scars to prove it. As cats go, he looked not unlike his canine namesake—same color, same torn ear. He had a doggish desire for human company and always answered to his name—also, as his hearing failed in old age, to Spencer Tracy, Count Basie, Edgar Cayce and Gracie Allen.

The day we collected Casey Jones the Second, I set out to teach him his name. I said it over and over. On the drive downtown to our place, holding him steady as his paws slid all over the seat: "Casey, it's okay." In our hallway: "Casey, you're home," seconds before he lifted his leg against the first chair in sight and drenched its taffeta skirt with a bright-yellow stream of urine (to my surprise, I didn't mind). In the living room: "No, Casey! Not on the carpet!" because he'd just lowered his butt there and I, unfamiliar with canine body language, thought he was about to take a dump. "Sometimes dogs just squat," said Paul.

Like Casey the cat in his prime, this dog could leap. The shower of kibble into his bowl sent him soaring with anticipation, his paws nearly tripping me between jumps. "Enough, Casey! Who do you think you are, Baryshnikov?"

I could have told him to sit; he must have learned that command in prison. But commands mean nothing to a dog unless the human knows how to use them. Besides, his happiness charmed me. No one in our household had jumped for joy since Ben was a preteen break dancer.

Preparing dinner that night, I found myself singing Casey's name. The song had no tune, the singer not much of a voice, and yet it was the sound of happiness. There came a soft, sudden thud: the freshly roasted pork tenderloin hitting the floor. "Oh, Casey! *No*, Casey!"

We ate the floor-seasoned tenderloin with a nice gewürztraminer while Casey lounged on his bed, listening for his name—his cue to sniff the chair legs for crumbs of our dinner. He was a little over a year old and hadn't even been born when we first embarked on our search. Perhaps I could have loved some other dog, had the right one appeared back then. But I couldn't imagine any dog more lovable than Casey. Dragging our feet would turn out to be the luckiest of breaks.

I've never liked admitting I was wrong, but the time had come. Tough little bugger that he was, Casey had pulled from me the apprehensive, irresistible excitement that only comes with starting an adventure. It was a feeling from the distant past: first night with Paul in the poky flat that felt wide as the world because it was ours; first time I held my baby and looked into his startling blue eyes; first trip to Paris, the only place I've been that looked exactly like the image in my mind, from the gargoyles of Notre Dame to the impossibly chic Parisians reading *Le Monde*. "You were right about getting a dog," I told Paul. "Let's keep Casey." When Casey thumped his tail, I decided to try an experiment: "Let's keep Spencer Tracy." More thumping from the pet bed. Same for all the variants: Count Basie, Dick Tracy, Edgar Cayce, Gracie Allen.

A family isn't a family without stories, private jokes and rituals. The stories and the jokes say, "This is who we are"; the rituals say, "This is how we do things." I was born into a family where tea was served at the appointed hour, in an antique pewter pot that my mother wheeled around on a teak cart from Denmark. When she died it came to us and found a new life as an end table piled with books, its backstory all but forgotten. If the tea cart was late, my father would start on the vodka that he stashed in various hidey-holes. Like all Maynard rituals, the tea routine applied a veneer of civility to my mother's futile campaign against chaos.

Paul and I had made a family where rituals are all about pleasure. We conclude every day in the same place: the TV couch, the one piece of furniture we'd happily share with our dog. When we first drew up our canine wish list, we didn't think to add "fits nicely between us on the middle seat cushion." The Newfoundland someone urged me to consider would have taken up too much space; the Havanese I thought I wanted would have claimed one lap or the other. Casey was the perfect size for stroking by us both as he slept.

If I couldn't tell the whole world about Casey, I'd settle for a Facebook post with two photos. The shot I took shows two jolly guys kicking back on the TV couch. They could be waiting for the Super Bowl to start—furry guy with his tongue hanging out, bald guy chuffed to be in such fine company. The second shot, snapped by Paul, sends a different message: woman meets visitor from another world. I'm bending over Casey, my hand barely making contact with his fur. What do I think he is, a Limoges teacup?

Everything about Casey held my attention. Brow-like tufts above his eyes. Coarse lashes, short as bristles for a doll's hairbrush (news to me that dogs have eyelashes). Contrasting toenails—outer ones black, inner ones creamy pink, like the moons of my own nails. Cinderella feet, long and narrow.

When I rolled him onto his back, he lifted his front paws in a pet-me gesture. I ran my fingers over the softest part of his coat. We called him ginger but in fact he was many shades of warm, from sand at high tide to the foamy heart on a latte. Show me who you are, my fingers said. Casey answered with a vigorous thump of his tail. Besides the torn ear, he had scars on all four legs. Liz had mentioned a dog fight on his journey north, a story that didn't ring true. You'd think the people who rescue dogs would know how to keep them safe. The scars gave him character, like stains and cuts on a harvest table handed down through the generations. My gaze wandered with my hands, returning to his eyes. Unlike any other eyes that ever met mine, they were almond-shaped with enormous pupils to get lost in.

The last time I touched a living creature with such devotional attention, I was powdering my newborn. He looked terrifyingly fragile, his outsize head a crushable blossom on a stalk of neck that would snap if I didn't watch out. At 22, I knew nothing about babies and never dreamed of having one so young. I felt unequal to the challenge ahead. Most important thing I'd ever do, according to everyone over 30. Compared to a newborn, Casey looked indestructible.

The phone rang: my sister Joyce, from California. She'd just found the photos on Facebook. "I've never seen that expression on your face before. You look cracked open." Joyce had known my face all her life, more than 60 years. She'd seen me withering, vengeful, conspiratorial and bored. Now and then, open to amusement with my kid sister. My expression was a marker of her standing in the world, so she monitored every nuance. That first day with Casey, I did look cracked open, and at least a decade younger.

As a teenager looking for love, I never guessed a dog would be the first coup de foudre of my life. With Paul I had asked, "Can I trust him?" With Ben, "Can I trust myself?" With Casey I held nothing back.

Many people can't resist a newborn's photo on Facebook. Even more can't resist a new dog's. My page lit up with good wishes. Lucky boy, lucky you, he's a beauty. Where did all these people come from? A long-lost friend volunteered to dog-sit; near-strangers cheered us on with photos of their own dogs. Word was out: A rescue mutt has landed at Rona's. Come one, come all.

I thought we were done with family-making. My photos told the truth: he was reconfiguring us as only a new family member can. Anyone could tell who Paul was to Casey—best pal and roughhousing partner. When Paul rubbed his belly, Casey's eyes rolled back in his head, his jaw dropped open and his whole body writhed in ecstasy. "Aw, Casey! *Aw, Casey!* What a guy!"

I hadn't heard that bellow since our son was a toddler, rolling and shrieking in his father's arms. Now I had two guys again, only this time one had four legs to wave in the air. I felt a bit like a hanger-on at a sports bar, mystified by a play that has everyone cheering. Casey and Paul had already discovered who they were to each other—the guys. Casey and I had not.

When Paul stepped out for a coffee, Casey whimpered at the door and prostrated himself there with a sigh audible across the room. When I took the garbage out, he didn't lift his head. In his world there was the Chosen One (Paul) and the Other One (me). Friends with dogs had told us this might happen. The Other One, they advised, should take charge of the food, the best way they'd found to narrow the affection gap. I had the power to set Casey dancing with joy, but only if I rattled his kibble can. Would I have no other role in his life? I found this mildly deflating, but I couldn't be jealous. After almost 45 years, I didn't think my husband could surprise me, but he had. All because of this fine dog we'd found.

Not long after Casey came to live with us, I had the strangest dream. I was 19 again and on the point of falling in love with the beautiful young man bending over me. I lay in a narrow bed, encased in a wetsuit. The young man sat beside me on a chair, naked to the waist—on the short side, neatly made, with a powerful chest and a fine head of ginger hair. Between his teeth he gripped the pull of the zipper that ran from my neck to my crotch. He had it open as far as my sternum. There he stopped and looked me in the eye. "I'm not sure how I feel about you."

"I'm not sure how I feel about you either." Exactly what I would have said at 19. I dreaded caring more for anyone than he cared about me, and consequently found myself alone until Paul decided we should be a couple. The man in my dream looked nothing like Paul, or anyone else I remembered. I woke feeling unsettled, as if a hulking trunk had been dragged from my emotional attic and left in the middle of the living room. Casey's arrival was so far a pure delight, the unlikeliest sort of moment for a dream of fear and disappointment, with a mystery man at its center.

Paul was still waking up when I recounted all the vivid details. "The whole thing was realer than reality. I could see the cabbage roses on the wallpaper."

In less than a minute Paul had the answer. "Ginger hair, smallish, neatly made, powerful chest. Sure sounds like Casey to me. Isn't it obvious?"

If Paul was right, I'd spent 65 years in an emotional wetsuit. I wanted him to be wrong. "That's not possible. A dream about Casey would be happy. I already know I love him." But I didn't know what loving Casey would ask of me. My waking self assumed it would be a straightforward matter do my share of the walking, keep the tenderloin out of his reach. My dreaming self understood that love is never straightforward. All day the dream flickered in my head while I went about my business. Then it let me go for a while.

Brain against Nose

On Casey's first morning I briefly forgot we had a dog. I padded out of bed, fuzzy with sleep, to find another creature sprawled on the TV couch. This had happened a good many times before, but in the past that creature was my husband, sleeping in the very spot where I meant to lounge with my second cup of coffee and the obituaries section of the *New York Times*. Paul sleeps best anywhere but the bed, and the TV tends to get him nodding in the small hours. His presence on the couch was essential for our TV series of the moment, but unwelcome in the tender hours of my awakening. The presence of a dog—our dog—was a marvel. *Oh, yes. It's you.*

He seemed to have expanded since the three of us curled up with *Grey's Anatomy*, two to watch and one to snore. In his languor, he pretty much filled the space, limbs every which way. His torn ear pointed straight up; the other flopped off the couch. Everything about him looked new. I perched on the ribbon of space he'd left me and stroked his flank. Up went all four paws, his way of wishing me good morning. And a fine morning it was, with Casey in it.

My notion of the ideal morning involved leisurely online perambulations in my bathrobe. At least it had until this day. But Casey needed his morning walk, which fell to me as the resident morning person. I couldn't be late, or he'd have an accident.

According to Liz, I should take him out right after breakfast. Liz had a fenced backyard; all she had to do was open the door. Then she could hang out in her PJs. Make a batch of muffins, do a crossword, call her mother. For me Casey's morning routine required lipstick, eyebrow pencil and presentable attire.

I'd laid everything out the night before—jeans and sweater for me, poop bags and liver treats for Casey. His crimson leash hung on the coat stand. I remembered Paul's first attempt at walking Casey, the circular stagger outside Liz's house. I was in for a challenge with this bruiser of a dog. Whoever trained him knew something Paul and I didn't.

In my editing days, I used to pull creative people into line. *No, you can't leave work when we're in crisis mode, summer hours be damned. You want to misspell a headline "because it looks better that way?" Go back to fourth grade.* After all the humans I'd tamed, how hard could it be to walk a dog? People did it while texting, hauling groceries, arguing into their cell phones and easing strollers over snowy curbs. The bolder ones did it on skateboards and bikes (surely not the safest technique, but they whizzed with panache). My neighborhood's fastest canine walker, a shepherd mix in an orange vest, scurried alongside a man on a scooter.

I cued the mental soundtrack for our walk, the Rolling Stones' saucy take on "Walking the Dog." As I muscled Casey out the door, a 50-years-younger Mick Jagger whooped, whistled and c'mon-c'mon'd in my head. *Show me how to do it, Mick! I know you're not singing about canines, but you're getting me in the mood to strut my stuff with Casey.*

We'd barely set out when a call rang out from behind, followed by a burst of laughter: "Who's walking who?" Good question. We couldn't seem to find our rhythm. Every few paces, a standoff ensued. My will against Casey's nose.

That nose. Low to the ground, sweeping the air, pulling us forward on a hellbent quest for anything that smelled edible. Down in one running bite went the soggy pizza crust, the nub of chicken in the gritty remains of its batter. Casey dragged me where the nose commanded, shoulders pumping. The exquisite precision of his nose recalled a hummingbird skimming a flower, yet the prize it sought might be the bloody feathers of a crushed pigeon or vomit from someone's drunken spree. No relic of a living or once-living creature was unpalatable to Casey.

When not busy prospecting for food, the nose evaluated spots for a pee. Casey zipped across the sidewalk, like a daredevil driver cutting through three lanes of traffic and came to a lurching stop at the hydrant summoning his nose. There he checked the accretion of canine pee before adding the finishing touch that proclaimed to the neighborhood dogs, "Casey was here!" He took his sweet time while a yellow rivulet spilled over the sidewalk and into the street. No matter how lavish the spray, he always had pee in reserve for the ritual known as marking.

For one with so much pee to offer, he could be stingy with the contents of his bladder. More than once, rump in line and leg hoisted, several previous angles found wanting, he declined to part with one golden drop of himself. This tree, this rusty fence, this pockmarked wall, which to me looked suitably disreputable, smelled all wrong to him. I'd shuffle my feet, then find myself scrambling to keep up with the orders of the almighty nose.

I thought I knew what it meant to walk my down-town neighborhood. Check out the movies playing at the local theater. Take note of a shoe sale, a new wood-oven pizzeria. Eavesdrop on conversations. All the while, set a pace, getting my exercise while my mind floated free. Walking was my gateway to an inner world in which I chose where to direct my attention. Not with Casey. I veered between meandering, waiting and a fair approximation of a drunken shuffle, both hands gripping the supposedly hands-free leash that looped around my waist (the dog walker's equivalent of training wheels).

Pedestrians swerved to avoid us; hazards loomed on every block. Casey tried to chase cars that looked wrong for unfathomable reasons (just when I thought it was only orange cabs that set him off, he'd charge at a black minivan). And that was the easy part. Squirrels sent him into warrior mode, with head-turning ululations and acrobatic leaps that nearly knocked me to the ground. Before Casey, squirrels reminded me adorably of Beatrix Potter's Nutkin. Now they seemed more like battle-hardened ruffians on *Game of Thrones*, a tribe of them always ready to burst from the nearest sapling.

Paul and I had a plan for Casey's walking, an hour a day from each of us. Why had I worried about Paul holding up his end, when I was the slight one trying to stay on my feet?

Flying at a squirrel I hadn't seen in time, Casey ran smack into a couple of pedestrians. The woman flashed a tolerant smile; the man scowled at me over his shoulder. At the rate we were going, someone might get hurt. Come to think of it, my shoulder was hurting already. I'd heard of strength training for golf and skiing, but dog walking?

I checked my watch. Five more minutes and we'd finish the hour. *We*. The right word for Casey and me on the couch, gazing into each other's eyes. Out on the street there wasn't any *we* or *us*. Intellect against instinct, that's what there was, intellect being the loser. We couldn't make it home fast enough. Just as I let my guard down, Casey had a set-to in the lobby with a neighbor's Lab, Betsy, infamous around the building for being caught roving the halls in the middle of the night. Her owner looked us both up and down, lip curled. "Rescue dog?" I mentioned the prison where Casey spent his puppyhood; surely it would lighten the mood. "You're brave," he said, pulling Betsy away from my jailbird.

The elevator seemed to crawl to the eighth floor. Casey ran to Paul's arms for some vigorous rubbing and the question that cannot be asked less than twice, with escalating volume: "Who's a good boy? Who's a *good boy*?"

We had a good boy, alright, but it soon became clear that we'd both have to up our walking game.

Paul got into trouble at St. James Park, beloved for its gazebo and landscaped gardens, when Casey had a noisy meltdown over a squirrel. A tweedy codger shook his finger at Paul. "That dog of yours is a nuisance. Don't you realize some of us come here for a little peace and quiet?" He pointed to a wisp of a dog that perched on its owner's lap like a stuffed toy on a satin pillow. "That's how a dog should behave. And until your dog gets the message, I suggest you keep him out of this park."

The night after Casey was exiled from the park, he lay on what we already called "Casey's couch," twitching as he snored. I ran my fingers along the cleft in his skull, where his ginger fur darkened to rust. A bovine skull has the same fundamental mammalian shape; I learned this from Georgia O'Keeffe, a painter at home with mystery. I'd never know for sure what Casey dreamed, but I figured a squirrel was involved. *Go, Casey, go. Run the varmint down.*

A dog trainer, Laurie, paid us a house call. She looked younger than our daughter would be if we'd gotten around to having one, but dog people on Yelp said she knew her stuff. I'd told her to expect a squirrel-crazed, trash-chomping rescue mutt, billed as a Lab-pug mix, although who could say for sure?

Laurie was sure. "He's all hound." With that pointy snout, he couldn't be anything else. And this explained a lot about our would-be assassin of squirrels. Like every hound who ever chased prey, Casey was designed for the task, with a nose that ranks among the wonders of the animal kingdom. His "squirrel attacks," as we called them, expressed his greatest gift. Some dogs were born to bark at strangers, ours was born to hunt rodents. I figured we had the better deal.

Laurie put Casey through a few paces. He sat, stayed, lay down as his convict had taught him in Ohio—and as he'd do for us, if we learned to speak his language. "You lucked out with this guy. He wants to please." He could have fooled me, but Laurie was the pro.

The three of us took Casey to a free-and-easy park where teens shot hoops. The neighbors kibitzing on benches wore anything and everything urban: hijabs and baseball caps, dreadlocks and magenta forelocks, skinny jeans fashionably ripped and baggy hiking pants. No one here would get fussed about a ruckus from a dog. The idea was for Laurie to watch Casey do his worst, and as we neared the first tree he rose—no, soared—to the occasion with his full repertoire of sound effects while I, the clueless human at the other end of the leash, stood by and bleated, "Casey, stop!"

I half-hoped Laurie would exclaim at his antics. If Casey had to raise hell, let him be the loudest, most epically acrobatic hell-raiser she had yet seen. How many squirrel-chasing dogs do backflips, then jump up to try again? For him the leash did not exist, nor did failure. Every squirrel was a promise of victory. Casey was my Don Quixote charging at windmills, my pratfalling Buster Keaton.

Laurie watched the show with her hands in the pockets of her hoodie; she'd seen every move before. "Like I said, all hound. You want his attention on you, not the squirrel. That's going to be your challenge. So let's get to work."

The Lauries of this world don't really train dogs. They teach perplexed humans to stop doing what doesn't work and acquire more constructive habits. Laurie reminded me a little of Annette, our couples counselor back in the striving years. Whatever long-forgotten muddle we were in, she'd seen it all before. How hard we worked with Annette in her basement office with the pine-paneled walls. How thoroughly we prepped for every session. If she'd given marks, we'd have aced her course. "You're remarkably well-matched," she once told us, peering through the enormous glasses women wore in the days of shoulder pads. "It's a miracle that you found each other." Her version of Laurie's "You lucked out."

With Annette we tuned in to the sometimes mystifying but basically well-intentioned people we were at heart. We were about to begin the corresponding process with a dog, who had never forgotten a birthday, stormed out in a huff or blamed either of us for a thing. Compared to making a marriage, training a dog should be a snap.

I wasn't getting through to Casey, Laurie said. My entreaties were meaningless noise, a sound soup of his name and half-hearted marching orders. Nature gave Casey a mission: slaughtering creatures who, in his mind, had no right to exist. To interrupt him, I'd have to make some noise. I had three options: whistling, shouting, a vigorous hand clap. I never learned to whistle, and clapping's no good with gloves on. That left shouting. As squirrel after squirrel romped by, I tried to summon a respectable shout: Casey! *Casey!*" How could it be that the name I loved to murmur was so hard to shout with conviction? Paul shook his head (in our class of two he was the star). Shouting had always come easily to him—too easily for my liking, but with dogs it served a purpose. "More authority," he said. "More volume."

The authority part I could nail. At 65 I'd damned well earned the right to be a feisty old dame. I demanded refunds with aplomb (and got them). I told waitstaff not to call me "dear" and shambling 20-somethings to make room for me on the sidewalk. I took issue with a startled female resident at the hospital emerg for introducing herself by her first name, thereby selling herself and other women short, when her name tag said she was a doctor. I complained and corrected. What I couldn't bear to do was shout.

Nobody loves a woman who shouts. In my neighborhood the only loud women are vacant-eyed crack addicts cursing the world. In my childhood home it was well understood that only my father had the right to shout and could erupt without warning. Sober, he quoted Yeats to my sister and me at bedtime. When we modeled new outfits with the price tags still attached, he would bow to us and ask, like a gentleman from an old movie, "May I have your telephone number?" (Telephone: an old-fashioned word, even circa 1960.) When he was drunk or hungover, the smallest thing could get him going—like the double boiler for his oatmeal. *What's become of the blasted thing? Is this any way to organize the kitchen cabinets?* The rest of us would wake to a percussion band of clatter. And I would know in the pit of my stomach that the day ahead was going to be a stinker.

Fear had a sound: shouting. What I feared was not so much my father's anger as my own. Because he was a man—the man of the house, in the language of those times—he got to blow off steam. Because I was a girl, I didn't. I should keep my head down, stay out of Daddy's way, do my best to placate this overgrown baby in the guise of a man.

Now I had Laurie's permission to shout. More than that, I had marching orders. For Casey's sake, I would learn to let it rip.

Becoming Us

After our first session with Laurie, I walked Casey with her voice in my head. I practiced shouting, "Hey!" when Casey jumped into predator mode. The pavement didn't split and swallow me up. I sounded loud and proud. Better yet, Casey started to get it—not every time or even half the time, but often enough, especially if I followed "Hey! Ca-a-a-SEY!" with a sharp tug on the leash. Then the treat, then the neck rub. "Good boy," I would say, as Laurie had taught me.

I was asking a lot of Casey. In the presence of a squirrel, he was anger incarnate. His eyes blazed; his hackles rose. I thought hackles were only an idiom until I saw the band of rage down Casey's back, where his fur is darker and coarser. When they stiffen, he looks bigger, more threatening. He wasn't my Don Quixote or my Buster Keaton, much as I liked to think so, but was an officer of natural law, determined to wipe lesser creatures from the earth. He objected to anyone scattering crumbs for squirrels that should have been tossed to him. Anger consumed him quickly but vanished with the squirrel. Casey's anger had an urgent purity. Unlike any human I'd known, he didn't hold grudges. He wouldn't ruminate on what he could have done to that squirrel if not for me, the spoilsport clutching the leash.

Casey and I started walking together as a biped and a quadruped, an aging woman and a young dog, a second-guesser and a creature of impulse. One who cleaned up, one who drooled on the floor. One who compared recipes for roasted Brussels sprouts, one who had to be restrained from licking barf off the sidewalk. It was the differences that held my attention then, not shared pleasure in the outing. Casey had his world, I had mine, and therefore I didn't think of him and me as us. I laughed when Paul said, of an excursion with Casey, "It took us forever to find parking, and then we had to park five minutes' walk from where we wanted to be." Come on, now. Casey looked for a parking space? He noted the walk time from the car to the dog park? Then I found myself speaking of the places I shared with Casey —our places, mine and his. The mural where I posed him for a shot, the park where we made friends with a juggler practicing his moves.

I was beginning to understand who we would be to each other. We were Us now, and it was enough. The unlikeliness of our comfort together magnified the joy of it. As long as squirrels roam the streets and parks of Toronto, there would be passing bursts of anger that didn't change a thing. What we had as a woman and a dog underscored the miracle of any two fallible beings, committed to opposing points of view, planting the stake in the ground that is Us.

Paul will be Paul, Rona will be Rona. In the beginning came a you, a me. One who slept late, one who equated purpose with rising early. One who left when Ben was a toddler, saying, "I never loved you" (me, exhausted by my young marriage and younger child), one who said, "It's not over. Let's try again." One who knew how things should be, one who didn't get it (actually, that would be both of us). From differences and disappointments, we created Us. And as Us, we brought Casey home.

Us-ness, once you've found it, can accommodate a fair bit of tension. Some days Casey and I were slightly off our game with squirrels number one through 17, but we'd get into the swing by squirrel 99. With a multitude of squirrels about, we always had another chance. I arrived at a grudging respect for the squirrels, who would stare Casey down with what looked to my human eyes like amusement. I'm not sure if squirrels are capable of amusement, but it pleased me to consider the matter. Squirrel by squirrel, day by day, we started to find our groove. We sometimes walked entire blocks without incident, Casey's tags clinking in time with my steps and his leash vibrating gently in my hand, now that I had given up my death grip. He knew every variation on our route. If I didn't pick his favorite, he would tug as if to ask, "You're sure about this?" I was sure. No big deal for a simpatico pair like us.

We were ripping through our value pack of poop bags. Casey was remarkably productive, often filling several bags in a single walk. Sultan of shit, Paul called him. Pasha of poop, pharaoh of feces. If we had to scoop, we might as well joke about it.

We fantasized about Casey as a future market leader who could bring in the bucks for Maynard Jones Enterprises. All he needed was a business plan. In a mock performance review, I laid out the problem: more flair than follow-through. "Casey, as your manager, I'm here to help you take your core competency to the next level. Let's talk about the resources you'll need going forward." I used to prize good conversation. Now I was performing skits on dog poop.

The one thing Casey's output would contribute to our household was a great deal of bowing and scraping. I didn't mind, though. Scooping gave me a chance to do one thing right every day. I might overcook the chicken, forget to call a friend, reread what I wrote yesterday and realize it has to go. But I could fill a green bag, if not two, with vile stuff that would otherwise seep into the watershed, contaminate the air or give children hookworm. This humble task literally grounded me. It forced me to tend the cracked and mottled sidewalk, the sodden leaves at the edge of a walking trail. It was a bondage I shared with all dog folk who care enough to do the right thing. The woman bending from her wheelchair with practiced caution, the elderly walker favoring a bad knee. The young parents exclaiming, as their toddler scooped for the family dachshund, "That's it! Good girl!"

I started walking Casey in early spring, when receding snow exposed a winter's worth of blackened excrement in every park. It clumped at the rims of hedges and dotted the sidewalks, a desiccated record of human can't-be-botheredness. So many scofflaws about, making me a target for those who hold dogs in contempt. Some people hate dogs for indiscriminate jumping, others for disturbing the peace with their barking. What unites them all is their loathing of poop.

I'd just disposed of Casey's first dump of the day when someone approached us with an open Clive Cussler novel in his hand and headphones blasting cacophony into his ears. As he passed, he yelled over his shoulder, "I hope it's not your dog who just left his business on the sidewalk! It's a pox on the city!" The last time I heard the word "pox" in the Shakespearean sense, I was watching *Romeo and Juliet*. Full points to Mr. Multitask for literary flair but his logic stung. He didn't turn his head when I called, "Not us!"

Us. Any scorn directed at Casey is really directed at me. When you get down to basics, I was scooping because I loved him. I hoped my fellow humans would look benevolently on him, or at least not disdain him. Every time I bent for Casey, I proved that Yeats was right: "Love has pitched his mansion in/ The place of excrement."

I no longer missed walking with Paul. Walking with a dog had distinct advantages. If Casey took any notice of my mood after a rough night's sleep, he showed no interest in what this meant for him or when I might snap out of it. He still sauntered beside me, ears sliding back to catch a rustle in the grass no human could detect. I didn't have to earn the good cheer that enveloped us both. Its engine was Casey's zest for the minutiae of his day—the stained wall that must be peed upon because no other wall compares, the postal clerk who must be greeted for a biscuit from her tin behind the counter. On Casey's map of pleasures, I was like the earth and the sky, reassuringly present but not the focal point.

As Laurie had taught me, I crossed the street to dodge cats, darting toddlers, unpredictable puppies—anything that might flip Casey's anger switch. He took exception to dogs off-leash (they made him feel insecure), dogs with enormous furry heads (not dogs, as far as he could tell) and a good many large black dogs (who knows?). Meanwhile other dogs took exception to him for similarly unfathomable reasons. When I couldn't remove Casey, I'd distract him by throwing a handful of treats about.

I can't say I remembered to ask on every block, "How safe is Casey going to feel here?" But in the early months we had a lot more fun when I did. Not since Ben learned to walk had I paid such close attention to another's experience of walking. I never entered Casey's mind and never will, but by making the effort I came close enough.

I knew we'd met a milestone when Casey had a full-throttle squirrel attack within pissing distance of where we first walked with Laurie. Loud, proud and fast, I executed my three-step routine: the shout, the tug, the "Good boy." Someone waved, a professional dog walker whose three charges were all sniffing the same patch of grass. "Nice work!" she called. How long had it been since I was asked, "Who's walking who?"

One morning we passed a sprig of a woman who was locked in a battle of wills with a huge and powerful boxer.

The dog wore one of those harnesses that supposedly prevent pulling, but it wasn't up to the job. A short leash didn't work either—the boxer seized it between his jaws. His massive haunches hung low, nearly grazing the sidewalk, as the woman hauled him one step forward with both hands, only to be yanked sideways. If he hadn't already sent her flying, he would do so any minute.

I watched them from across the street, hoping they were almost home. "It gets easier!" I'd have called, if I thought she could hear me over the traffic and the pounding of her own heart and the how-did-I-get-into-this voice in her head. Soon enough she'd see for herself. She too would be Us with a dog.

I had a brainwave: Us-ness might serve a practical purpose. Casey has the enviable canine gift for sleeping anyplace he happens to be, from the back seat of the car to a friend's yard. I have the human gift for rolling worries around in my brain when all I crave is sleep. In the middle of a restless night, I went looking for a soporific book and found Casey zonked out on the TV couch. He didn't stir when I sat down beside him to stroke the soft fur on his neck. He exhaled, sinking deeper into his rest. He sounded almost human, but then every human sigh is mammalian. *Hey, Casey. Take me with you.*

He'd left me just enough room to curl up on the couch and make his firm, warm chest my pillow. Unlike all other pillows in my life, Casey's chest expands with his breath. His fur smells pungently of himself. No matter what he's kicked up on our rambles or where he's pushed his snout, he would smell exactly as he does. My headful of niggles rose and fell with Casey's breath like a boat on a calm sea. I didn't yet know I was taking liberties. An 11-pound human head is a not-inconsiderable burden for the chest of a medium-size dog, and any dog hates to be confined. But Casey was too far gone to throw me off right away. He supported me for about five breaths, enough to remind me how deep and slow a breath can be. I'll never paint like Matisse or write a poem like Emily Dickinson, but Casey let me believe that I could sleep like my personal master of the art.

For the sleep of my dreams, I'd gone to extraordinary lengths. Bought a king-size mattress certified by NASA and developed from materials used in space research. Followed a regime of pre-bedtime baths and stretches. Taken heavy-duty sleeping pills. Consulted a sleep psychiatrist to help me kick the habit and learn the rules of "more efficient sleep." In a beige box of a room with nothing on the walls but diplomas, he gave me my marching orders. No clock watching. After 20 sleepless minutes I should get up and read until I started to nod. This puzzled me: "If I can't look at the clock, how am I supposed to know when my 20 minutes are up?" I might as well have asked how to hear the sound of one hand clapping. His blank expression said, "Figure it out," and after a fashion I did. On his detox program I yawned my way through all 615 pages of *The Children's Book*. Five years later, I still hadn't found a literary sleep aid to equal A.S. Byatt.

In the half-light of an early spring morning, I found Casey dead to the world. What he knew about sleep, no human could teach me.

The most important thing to do for restful sleep, with abandon, is nothing. If I had any gift for doing nothing, I would not have spent years on the hunt for the Project. Yet falling asleep, like falling in love, is about letting go of expectations, loosening your grip on control. I learned this watching Casey sleep. He put that psychiatrist to shame. Sprawled or curled nose to tail, eyes shut or half open, he gets the average dog's 12 to 14 hours a day. All I asked was seven. With a little help from my canine coach, I'd become a whole new sleeper.

It didn't occur to me then that he could coach me better in the bed, at my side. Roughly half of dog people sleep with their animals, but I'd made a rule—no dirty paws on our 300-thread-count sheets—and I was sticking to it. Back in the bedroom, the sheets had cooled while I hung out with Casey. My side of the bed looked like the shipwreck of my night so far—a tangle of sheets, eyeshades and layers of clothing added, then subtracted in my search for the right body temperature. Paul's side lay untouched while he slept in his favorite armchair. I positioned myself on the neck-cradling pillow I take with me everywhere. The white-noise machine whirred. I replayed the moment Casey and I had just shared—his fur against my cheek, his breath lifting me—until I slipped into a dream of Us.

Dog People

"So," said a friend of a friend, whom I'd known for all of three minutes. "I hear you've adopted a dog. Are you cooking for him yet?"

Hell, no. What a wild idea. On top of all the meals I already cooked from scratch for Paul and me—tongue-of-fire beans soaked overnight for baking because navy beans didn't cut it, only the best Parmesan and dried porcini for my white Bolognese—I should be cooking for Casey? It had crossed my mind that by easing up on all my stirring and slicing, not to mention the shopping, I could gain enough time to read *Middlemarch*, brush up on my French and never miss the dried porcini. Besides, if Casey had his way, he'd dine on rotting trash (as Paul tells it, Casey invented the best-after date). No, I wouldn't be cooking organic beef stew for Casey. "Kibble seems to suit him just fine," I said.

"You'll be cooking for him before you know it. When you're ready, I've got a great recipe. It's done wonders for my boy Harley. People stop me on the street to admire his coat."

It's not as if Casey was eating junk kibble. He'd already had an upgrade from the no-nonsense brand that had sustained his feline namesake. He could demolish a bowlful in half a minute, tops. But as Laurie wrapped up a training session, she caught sight of the jumbo bag of Science Diet and suggested we might want to make a change. She could tell from our built-in wine racks and collection of stained cookbooks that we didn't take eating lightly. "I'm not saying there's anything wrong with Science Diet. But seriously, would *you* want to eat a meal called 'Science'?"

There are moments when I know what Paul is thinking and can sense him reading my mind. We don't even have to look at each other, although this time we did, awakened to our own cluelessness. Science Benedict for brunch? No way. Science pie? Sounds like a middle-school project. And Laurie wasn't done building her case. Our dog would get bored with the same old meal twice a day. Her dogs liked a brand that comes in many flavors, from surf and turf to game bird. "Plus, it's grain-free," she added, as if we wouldn't dream of letting grains go down Casey's gullet.

The idea that dogs should not eat grains was news to us, although many vets, including our own, had already dismissed it as a marketing ploy. But who were we to argue with a dog maven like Laurie? I loaded up on the recommended brand, prettily packaged with a plump red apple in the logo (no blemished fruit for Casey). Each flavor had its own bright palette, turning an armload of bags into a lumpy bouquet that crackled when I walked. At the sight of me, a condo neighbor asked, "Is that designer coffee?"

"Gourmet dog food. Grain-free." My neighbor looked at me as if I'd lost my mind.

Not long after Casey's arrival, I caught up with my friend Ellen, my first mentor in all things dog. "There's nothing like dog love," she had promised. "It'll change your life." Ellen nodded along as I told her, in fulsome detail, how right she'd been. When I ran out of Casey news to babble on about, she posed the most surprising question: "So what do you call yourself?"

Call myself? Rona, what else? Never Ro. If Ellen planned to start calling me Ro, I'd have to set her straight right now.

"I mean, what are you to Casey?"

"His owner, of course."

My friend looked downcast. She's too kind to give me a lecture, but I got the point. You own your washer and dryer, not the family member who happens to have four legs.

"Well, I'm also Casey's human. How about that?"

She brightened but she still wasn't with me. Ellen calls herself Teddy's mom, Teddy being a winsome 14-pound golden doodle. She clearly has the weight of public opinion on her side. I was "mom" to Dr. Bob at the animal hospital, the local pet-food purveyors and our dog trainer, along with any number of random dog folk. "Mom" everywhere but in my own mind and Paul's. (He liked to call us Casey's "peeps.")

"Mom is more intimate," Ellen said. "My daughter likes to call herself Teddy's mom too, but that's my role. Only one woman gets to be mom."

"One person gets to be my child," I told Ellen. "Person, not dog. That's Ben. As far as I'm concerned, Casey's mom is a bitch in Ohio."

I didn't mean to sound harsh. I had only warm feelings for Casey's mom. Yet to call Casey my child would be to deny both the otherness of him and the distinctive sense of ease I found with him. All we had to do was feed him, walk him and let him be our good boy because that's all he'll ever want to be (although Exterminator-in-Chief of Rodents would make an attractive sideline). He would not be our legacy. We were preparing him for nothing more than another day like this day, and another and another after that.

I never guessed I had it in me to become a dog person. Before I saw the light, I was one of those "just a dog" people. I didn't understand what use a dog could have for a daycare center, a turtleneck sweater with faux leather buttons or fish-skin nuggets imported from Iceland, all of which we provide for Casey. When a colleague took time off work to mourn her dog, I thought her grief diminished the more worthy dead: humans. It's not as if your late dog ever took you out for dinner on your birthday or helped you figure out how to get more respect at the office. Besides, you could get another dog. I wished I could tell that long-ago colleague, whom I haven't seen in years, "I'm sorry for judging you. I've changed."

As a dog person, I joined a tribe, a motley bunch. Breeders dedicated to their standards, rescue advocates convinced that to purchase a purebred dog is to sentence a deserving mutt to death. The home-cooking crowd and homeless people who give their dogs first crack at any food they can scavenge. Instagrammers whose dogs wear sunglasses and designer fedoras, purists who insist that dogs should look like dogs. Members of the tribe have their fierce disagreements, but they stand united on this: Beloved dogs deserve the same stature as the most beloved humans. Until they're sure you understand the core principle, you remain a provisional member.

Halfway through a walk with Casey, I heard a high, sharp voice from behind: "Excuse me! Please don't slap your dog!" She couldn't have been more than ten.

"I didn't slap him. He was going nuts over a squirrel, so I clapped my hands to get his attention. A dog trainer taught me. See? He's not jumping anymore."

Invoking a higher authority didn't get me far with this girl. She pursed her lips and glared. "All the same, if you were a dog, I don't think you'd want to be slapped."

"You bet I wouldn't. That's why I don't slap him. But it's great that you look out for animals."

I liked her, censorious child that she was. The bookishness of "all the same," the gumption to challenge a sexagenarian. As with grownup dog people, her excesses underscored the strength of her devotion. Besides, I had excesses of my own. My bookshelf overflowed with dog memoirs, dog lore, dog psychology and "Dr. Spock for dogs." I drew the line at *How Smart Is Your Dog?*, but only because it didn't contain an IQ test.

I became a student of dog cartoons (dog to psychiatrist, who lies weeping on the couch: "Well, *I* think you're wonderful"). I pounced upon headlines about hero dogs, service dogs, plucky street dogs and dogs whose unlikely interspecies friendships became parables to me. Rex, the formerly vicious German shepherd, shared his bowl and bed with Geraldine the goose. (He was facing euthanasia, she calmed him just in time.) Never one to follow celebrity news, I made an exception for celebrity dogs. Joaquin Phoenix was cooking sweet potatoes for his vegan dogs; the Queen's corgis dined on freshly skinned rabbits killed on her lands and cooked in a pot kept boiling on the stove (this according to their profile in *Vanity Fair*, which I could practically quote by heart). Critics panned *A Dog's Purpose*; I had to see it right away—and wept on cue, reveling in surrender to the purest treacle.

I no longer hankered to climb to Machu Picchu, where the air is thin and bathrooms nonexistent past the entrance; Dog Mountain was more my speed. At Dog Mountain in St. Johnsbury, Vermont, we could walk Casey on trails out of Grandma Moses and honor departed dogs in the chapel, its walls a collage of tributes left by dog people from all over. We'd passed St. Johnsbury on any number of New England road trips. Next time I'd say, "Let's go to Dog Mountain."

Paul only meant to talk me into a dog, but he made me a shameless dog person. Though when it came to dogs, he could be pretty shameless himself. One morning I found him catching up with the news of the world, with that smile he gets when whatever he's just noticed is so transportingly comical, he's torn between immediate sharing and a few seconds more of private pleasure. He must have seen a biting political cartoon. Skullduggery in high places, the poor trampled by the powerful, a deluge of awfulness ripe for mockery. He stroked his beard, then looked up from his iPad. "Have you seen the video of the dog who takes herself sledding?"

I bent to watch it again. Friend after friend had shared that video on Facebook, yet every time it felt new. Plucky sheepdog drags a sled up a hill, flies down, starts all over again, an endless loop of happiness. "How about the dog body-sliding down a hill? So smart, he's figured out he doesn't need a sled." Old news to Paul, who already had the window open. He must have meant to do something useful. Pay some bills, pick up the dry cleaning. Then he found himself hooked by a video that linked to more of the same. He'd crossed the boundary that separates the human world, with its outrages and obligations, from the happier realm we had entered with Casey.

I christened it the Doggy Dog World, tipping my hat to Anonymous for a term I wish I'd dreamed up myself. "Doggy Dog World" is an eggcorn, a weirdly evocative misapprehension of a common word or phrase, "eggcorn" being both example and inspiration. Someone misheard "acorn," noticed the nut's egg shape and started a movement among collectors of linguistic oddities. Eggcorns can be poetic ("star-craving mad," "on tender hooks"), comically appropriate ("nip it in the butt") or ploddingly literal ("old timers' disease"). While most of them at least approximate the original, "Doggy Dog World" subverts it, kicking up the sourness of "dog eat dog" like so much dirt in the dog park. In the Doggy Dog World, there's always good news to find and pass on.

Before Casey, we only reminisced about our lives. *Remember when Ben said he'd give up his birthdays so he could have an older brother? Remember when we rented the "secluded cottage on a stream" that turned out to be a yurt in the middle of a mosquito-infested swamp? And left on arrival because you refused to stay?* "You" being Paul, who convinced me to strike out on a road trip up the Maine coast—a great idea, it turned out—instead of hunkering down in the yurt for fear of wasting money.

I never guessed I would come to ask my husband, "Remember the world's worst sheepdog?" That would be Nelson, the viral sensation who leads his flock on a merry chase that resembles an interspecies circus act, 35 seconds of mind-clearing zaniness.

"If Casey were a sheepdog, that's who he'd be," Paul said. At the sound of his name, Casey slapped the chair leg with his tail. All canine conversations circled back to him, and every dog video awakened thoughts of him—if not because it featured Casey-ish hijinks, then because it showed the opposite, a level of quasi-human cleverness we hadn't detected in Casey. Eclipse, a Lab-mastiff mix, took the bus to the park by herself, winning over both the driver and the passengers. Stanley the Airedale "sang" on the phone when his owner said, "Tell me you love me."

The most I could expect from Casey on a bus is that he wouldn't trip anyone, and as for the phone, he didn't have a clue. He had come to believe that if it rang when Paul was out, then the call could only be from his Chosen

One, requesting Casey's presence on an outing to the Cherry Beach dog park. He would tear through our condo, galloping and spinning, ready for me to leash him up and take him down to the waiting car (beachmobile to him).

More likely Paul was calling from the grocery store, seeking guidance on which cleaning spray to buy. On a typical grocery run, he'd make a flurry of calls to verify the finer points of my shopping list, each call rousing Casey to greater heights of ecstasy. "You're getting him terribly excited," I told Paul. Could he not take a flyer on the Greek yogurt? Did he have to keep calling for advice?

He couldn't and he did. Casey's whirligig routine was too entrancing for us both, and me in particular. As a child of three or four, I too would get carried away by excitement, running and spinning and flapping my arms. I don't remember these outbursts, only my mother's accounts of their disconcerting expressiveness. Unless I learned to calm down, I'd be a laughingstock. I got the message, but now I had a dog to run and spin for me. On his hind legs he even flapped his paws.

Things We Do for Love

Paul came home from the cardiologist's office feeling chuffed. The doctor liked his blood pressure numbers. Had Paul lost weight?

"I wish," said my husband. "I've been walking a dog."

That he had, an hour a day, as promised. If weather cut the outing short, he kept track of every minute he "owed" Casey. So much for my fear that he couldn't or wouldn't hold up his end. His cane still hung on our coat rack, barely visible amid the hats and jackets.

What a person does for love is a sacrifice freely chosen. It requires no reminders from anyone else. The real surprise was all the little sacrifices loving Casey asked of us. Things that used to be spur-of-the moment now demanded meticulous planning. For instance, an afternoon movie.

In the old days, we might have made an evening of it. Stopped at a bar for cocktails, wandered into the first restaurant with a decent Yelp rating and a table for two. Casey made short work of that, but by thinking ahead we could still keep up with new releases. I was double-checking

70

the time of our show when the phone rang, Paul's mobile number on the screen. Calling from the car, I assumed, to tell me he'd be home in five. (He was already running late.) No, he was still on the walking trail with Casey. "We've had a poop emergency. Long story."

The two of us had scripted every minute of this movie date. Paul would swing by and wait in the car while I whisked Casey upstairs and settled him with a fresh bowl of water. We'd be off in a flash, might catch a few trailers unless we hit every red light. Now Paul said he had to shower first. He was bending to pick up after Casey when his cap blew off in mid-scoop, one of those moments when a dog walker needs a third hand. Grab the cap, tie the bag, hold the leash before the dog breaks free. Next thing you know, you've got poop on your fingers and everything else you touch. Which, as you flail, might be your head. At the moment when you should be pulling out of the driveway, your wife is checking your pate for suspicious brown stains—and rechecking when none turn up.

So much for the show. The next one would conflict with the 5:30 dog walk, followed by dinner preparations. How important was this movie, anyway? We'd curl up with Casey and watch *The Americans* at the time of our choosing. One of us would stroke his hindquarters, the other the fur around his neck. Sometimes we held hands on his trunk as his chest rose and fell. On TV Elizabeth Jennings, a Russian spy in the guise of a suburban working mother, made the calculation that a hapless innocent knew too much and dispatched her with a broken vodka bottle. On the couch Casey chased squirrels in a dream.

What a good boy he was. I heard about a rottweiler, terrified of horses, who would hurl himself at the TV if one appeared. Casey reacted to nothing. From the Arsenal game to *I Love Lucy*, it was all background for a snooze. The exception was a single scene of *Dogs*, the six-part Netflix documentary. Early one morning on Lake Como, a fisherman blows a whistle for his Lab. The TV dog, thick with age, comes running to the boat, frisky as a pup. Our dog jumped from the deepest of slumbers to see who required his assistance. If anyone had ever blown a whistle for Casey, we had no idea who it was. His prisoner, maybe? Until that moment we knew where TV was taking us—a fishing village in Italy. The whistle took Casey somewhere known only to himself and left us momentarily on shore, mystified by *The Casey Show*.

I forget most of what I watch with random strangers in the dark. I'll remember that whistle for as long as I have a memory. "Pay attention," it told me. "You think you understand the ones you love. Don't give yourself any airs."

I've learned to tell my husband, with studied calm, "What I think I hear you saying is . . ." I like to hear this back, or some version of it. And yet, after a lifetime of marriage, I can't always tell when Paul is joking. I might complete a sentence for him, only to be reproved: Not only did I interrupt him, he had meant to make a different point altogether. I couldn't let go of the conviction that a failure of understanding is a failure of love. Sometimes it's more like a miracle. You don't and can't understand, but here you are. Loving.

Casey sat waiting for his orders. Ears pricked, tail lifted. I asked Paul, or maybe he asked me, "What do you suppose is going on in his head?"

Answer: "I haven't the faintest idea."

We didn't need to know. We had the wonder. We shared it.

Perfect

All we knew about Casey was what Liz had told us—the prison, the shelter, the bewildering label "Lab-pug mix." Who was this extraordinary mutt from Ohio, who'd somehow made his way to us, when so many other people might have snapped him up? If we'd bought our dog from a breeder, we'd know the whole story. We'd carry a picture in our minds of where he came from. *This is the meadow. This is the puppy playroom. These are the people who raised our dog and his adorably photographed parents.* As it was, we'd brought home a mystery.

Well-meaning strangers offered theories. "Looks like you've got yourselves a Rhodesian ridgeback," said a condo neighbor, overlooking the absence of a ridge. "Is that a Caribbean potcake dog?" asked a passerby who'd adopted a near-twin to Casey—and proceeded to educate me on potcakes, the mixed-breed strays that get their name from the rice and peas that stick to the bottom of the pot. A group of them is called, charmingly, a parliament. Such arcane things you learn while walking a dog. I liked the thought of Casey in a parliament, but the islands are a long way from Ohio. We'd never know whether Casey was born in a basement or a barn, the runt of the litter or the sturdiest, but science could tell us quite a bit about the mélange of breeds that made him the dog we adored. The moment had arrived for Casey's DNA test.

I should have seen it coming, given Paul's longstanding fascination with family history and DNA testing. He'd already overseen several tests of our own. Casey's would double as initiation into our family. For $85 Paul ordered a kit from a reputable player in a dauntingly crowded field. He swabbed the inside of Casey's cheek. We waited while the scientists at Wisdom Panel compared the DNA in our dog's saliva to samples from more than 250 breeds and traced our dog's ancestry back three generations. A seven-page report came back. More beagle than anything else, jots of Boston terrier and bulldog. Not a trace of Lab or pug. Liz had been blowing hot air, and Laurie knew less than she thought.

To us Casey just looks like Casey. He has smaller ears than a beagle and none of the characteristic markings. But beagle aficionados have stopped me on the street to ask, "Is that a beagle mix?" Casey has a tribe and by extension it is our tribe too.

When I first went looking for the perfect breed, I ruled out a beagle. Hard to train, said the doggy websites. Always running off in search of prey. Just like Casey (Dogtime.com gives beagles five stars for "wanderlust potential"). One intoxicating day in early spring, I set him free in a park to chase a tennis ball. With a seemingly vast expanse of meadow between us and a busy street, it didn't feel like much of a risk. My underhanded throw had not improved since gym class, but he humored me for a while. He gamboled at half his running speed, I plodded and puffed. The ball didn't soar, it sank. I was already winded when Casey took off in pursuit of a scent, barely making contact with the ground. He had never looked more graceful, a vanishing streak of ginger whose speed thrilled and terrified me. I stumbled after him, waving a dried-out liver treat. I had once been an ungainly runner, but bad knees had forced me to quit. Whatever made me think I should attempt to play fetch in an unfenced park with a hunting hound in his salad days?

As Casey bolted past a construction site, a worker yelled, "Somebody catch that dog!" Somebody did, just in time—a hard-hatted version of Casey, his biceps ready for the cover of *Men's Health*. "Better watch this guy," he said, like one familiar with guyish excess. As I leashed Casey up, I pictured him bloody and limp in my arms. He'd been ours for a matter of months, and already I'd almost lost him.

I asked dog people for advice. One friend urged me to double down on Casey's training. Another told me to accept his headstrong nature. "Typical beagle," she explained, having lived with a few. "Takes commands under advisement. Answers your call if he's got nothing more exciting to do. Remember, he was born to follow his nose. For his own good, keep him on the leash."

One evening Paul saw Casey chase a gaggle of rabbits onto the active railroad track abutting a park. He'd followed them through a hole in a chain-link fence. Paul, stranded on the other side, brandished a crumpled bag of treats while waiting for Casey to choose a sure thing over the rabbits. Could we risk letting him die on the mission nature gave him? Were we capable of saying with conviction, "He was doing what he loved?" We couldn't and we weren't. After the rabbit fiasco, we couldn't trust Casey off-leash except inside a fence he couldn't leap or wiggle through.

We tallied up the guesses and half-truths that had comprised Liz's pitch for the dog then known as Tucker. "Dignified" (had she seen him near a squirrel?). "Hardly sheds" (all relative, I guess). "Thirty pounds." On the scale at Dr. Bob's, Casey weighed in at 40, most of it muscle. His first feat of strength, pulling us in circles outside Liz's house, was a warmup for the mayhem he caused when he tagged along with Paul to the podiatrist's office. "I love dogs," said the podiatrist, who'd raised a few. "Just tether him to my desk." Casey had no interest in sitting by the desk. When the instruments clinked, he must have thought treats were on offer. In his eagerness, he broke the desk. (The podiatrist, a dog man to the core, refused to let Paul pay for the damage.)

Liz told only one whopper that stung: "great with kids." If only. I'd always thought kids and dogs were like Lassie and Timmy, meant to be together. In fact there are dogs who feel anxious around small, impulsive humans, and Casey is that kind of dog. Some kids approached him politely and asked, "May I pet him?" Their parents had warned them that a frightened dog may bite. Casey hardly distinguished between well-schooled children and the ones who pointed and hopped like windup toys. Either way he growled and stiffened. We came up with a story for the crestfallen children, one that sounded vaguely true. "Sorry, he's scared of kids. He used to live in a prison, and he never saw kids there. Bet you never guessed a kid like you could be scary." The children's eyes grew wide. They craved more details about Casey's life behind bars, but it only took a minute to recount what little we knew.

The child who scared Casey most was our six-year-old grandson, who'd been asking for a dog of his own and hoped ours would be an affectionate stand-in. Things went badly from the start. Casey resented this dog-size creature with the nerve to displace him on the sofa cushion next to the Font of all Goodness ("Grandpa" to Cameron). Finding Paul and Cameron side by side, Casey would launch himself at them in a frenzy of licking and wagging, as if to say, "Mine! Mine!" Cameron's response to this never varied: "Casey's going to bite me!"

I tried to explain that Casey was just jealous. "He loves Grandpa most in the world and me a bit less. He needs time to get to know you."

We did our best to help the two make friends. *Hey, Cameron, how about throwing Casey a ball? Give him a blueberry, Cameron—he loves blueberries. That's right. Now give him another one.* After doling out a handful of blueberries, Cameron asked me, "Does Casey love me a little?"

"I think he's coming around." I'd been wrong about this before, but maybe this time would be different. If I'd known the basics of canine body language, I might have detected warning flags: ears pulled flat against his head, lips curled back, whites of his eyes enlarged. I might have headed off the snarl, and the tears that followed.

Casey never did bite Cameron. Many balls and blueberries along, each still expects to be anxious in the presence of the other. They have reached a truce, but they still aren't friends. In search of hope, I consulted Patricia McConnell's blog, *The Other End of the Leash*. If anyone knows how to bring a child and a dog together, it's McConnell, a dog trainer and author with a well-earned reputation for authority. She laid it on the line: "Every dog is different, and some dogs will never be comfortable around kids, period."

As the truth about Casey and kids sank in, I asked Paul, "Isn't it for the best we didn't know?" Probably so, he concluded. The Lab-pug canard was a mere detail, the shedding a minor inconvenience, Casey's size and strength a manageable challenge. But when it came to the matter of friendliness to children, and one child in particular, neither of us would have compromised. We'd have wanted a more suitable dog than the one who now seemed indispensable.

Yet despite everything Liz got wrong about Casey, she was right about the one thing that mattered: He was the perfect dog for us. And oddly enough, what made him perfect was the difference between the checklist dog we thought we were getting and the real, sometimes baffling dog we'd brought home.

Not a day passed when one of us did not exclaim, "Casey, you're a complication!"—always spoken with a little irritation and a lot of gratitude for how bearable the complications were. It became a one-line love song, treasured because no one but ourselves could sing it, and with every repetition we celebrated love itself. No complications, no Casey.

"I'm not one for regrets," Paul said, "but sometimes I think of all the other dogs we could have loved before Casey."

"Being our first is part of Casey's specialness. He's our starter dog. The one who shows us what living with a dog is all about."

I caught myself. At our age, we wouldn't have a dynasty of dogs to love. Maybe one more, if we were lucky. But another dog could only mean the loss of Casey. How could we call that luck? Jeanette's warning came back to me—"Remember, this will be a ten-year commitment." Ten years: the difference between ankle socks and nylons, fighting with my mother and becoming a mother, moving into the big corner office and handing in my key. I was hoping for more than ten years with Casey, which would bring us close to 80 if not all the way there. He might be our first and last.

The Caravaggio Chair

We came home from a play to find Casey enthroned in my mother's rose velvet armchair. It was still hers to me, although she'd been dead for 26 years. Casey filled the seat from arm to arm—tail brushing the creamy piping, head against the raw silk throw cushion. The chair had never looked more impressive than it did occupied by a ginger dog. For once he made no move to greet us at the door. That would mean ceding the space he'd claimed. But rules were rules, and my mother's chair was off limits. I clapped my hands and down he went, not quickly.

We'd been blessed with a dog we could trust with the run of the house. He wouldn't chew a hole in the wall, rip the sofa cushions apart or devour the contents of the fridge. As Laurie had said, he wanted to please. Yet in a spot for a solitary nap, he also wanted softness and a prime view of the door. Only my mother's chair gave him both. We hardly ever caught him there; he was wily enough not to trespass except when we were out. Flecks of fur gave him away, along with a worn patch that seemed to be expanding.

There are sprays to keep dogs off the furniture, but I had a better idea. The next time we left Casey on his own, I placed our largest and most beautiful coffee-table art book on the chair, *Discovering Caravaggio*. We came home to find it still in position. On the cover St. Matthew takes dictation from an angel, his swirling burgundy robe complementing the rose velvet upholstery. How elegant they looked together, this book and this chair. It pleased me that our scamp of a dog had been foiled by Western art's most infamous reprobate, a murderer who died in exile with a price on his head.

That day my mother's chair became the Caravaggio chair.

Maybe every family has a private lexicon. Our own harks back to our son's childhood. Ben forgot long ago that he ever inquired about today's "tempshitter" or did anyone "a favorite," so these terms now belong to us alone, part of our essential Us-ness. It's not so easy for a dog to bequeath any words to a household, but Casey had done it. At least one baffled visitor asked, scanning our rumpled living room for sleek designer furniture from an Italian showroom, "You have a Caravaggio chair?"

The Caravaggio chair was seafoam green wool when my mother selected it for the grand white colonial house that was known in the family as Maynard Hall. She and my father had stretched to buy the place and together they turned it into a museum of sorts for his paintings. My father's art required a setting of distinction; mass-produced maple wouldn't do.

My mother set her sights on Danish teak, unavailable then at any store in the area. She had to order what she wanted from Denmark, one piece at a time. When the dining room table arrived with too prominent a grain for her liking, she sent it back and waited for another. To acquire a collection of what was then called Danish Modern, she bought all her clothes on sale and wrote more articles for glossy magazines, her typewriter clacking while the brisket simmered.

My mother had an agent in New York and made more money than my father, forever the lowest-paid man in his department. (There were no women.) For a while he made wistful noises about a La-Z-Boy, but my mother called the shots on decor. Her Danish chairs were for sipping sherry and reading John Updike. Joyce and I learned early to treat them like persnickety guests. Our dog Nicky never tried his luck on those chairs.

Casey did more damage in a couple of months than Paul and I could do in a lifetime, but *Discovering Caravaggio* kept him at bay. It didn't seem like any accident that this book, of all the books that crammed our shelves, should be the one with protective powers. I had bought it in memory of a trip to Rome, where we discovered Caravaggio. In the chapel of San Luigi dei Francesi, his monumental paintings on the life and death of St. Matthew blazed like a personal message from the master. One painting in particular: the moment that changed Matthew's life. And the time had come for me to change my own, mired as I was in the what-now doldrums of retirement, a word I loathed. "I'm in my discovery years," I would say, the new version of "I'm going to surprise myself." But no matter where our travels took me, I always came home to the unmet challenge of the

Project. What would I do with myself? How did people change their lives, anyway? *The Calling of Saint Matthew* showed me how one man changed his.

The unawakened Matthew was a sinner and a sellout, a tax collector engaged in the oppression of his fellow Jews. In the fresco he sits among his richly dressed cronies, a scattering of coins on the table. High above the money grubbers' heads, a window looks out on a mud-colored sky. The one source of light is an unseen door, and in it stands a stranger: Christ, his illuminated profile young and grave, his hand weathered. A workingman's hand, pointing at the startled Matthew, who in turn points to himself. I can hear him thinking, *Me? Now? You must be looking for some other guy.* Christ is barefoot; Matthew wears a consequential hat and satin sleeves that flow onto the table. Minutes from now, he'll leave vanities behind. He flinches, pulling away from Christ, but his wide eyes are already following, a perfect rendition of conflict nearly resolved on the boundary between one life and another.

Matthew met his lord and savior; I met a dog. Matthew would be martyred for changing; my change had cost me a lot of fur, some afternoon movies and a little damage to a chair. So far I was getting off lightly. I couldn't see any better than Matthew what the future held, but the present hadn't felt so good in ages. Perhaps a more upbeat frame of mind would bring the Project into view.

One night I forgot to shield the chair before leaving Casey on his own. I promised myself I would remember from then on, but I didn't. The worn patch became a giant smudge where he'd destroyed the nap of the velvet. My mother would shake her head at the decline of standards on my watch.

Not that I was giving up. The book would still join the silk cushion as an accessory of the chair. To sit there, all I had to do was move *Discovering Caravaggio*. It seemed so easy. Convenient, even. With the book already in my hands, I could take another look at *The Calling of Saint Matthew*.

Then I got tired of shuffling the book between the coffee table and the chair. Why bother with this anymore?

The pasta water was coming to a boil. Around me lay the familiar clutter of home. Paul's latest Michael Connelly thriller, a flyer from the Art Gallery of Ontario. Throw cushions flattened from being slept on by a man who has trouble sleeping in a bed. A slightly faded posy with a few days left. My splayed copy of Mark Strand's collected poems, open to "Five Dogs," in which canine stand-ins for the poet muse on life, death and art. From where I sat, I couldn't see the drool Casey left on the TV couch when he made a cushion fort and rested his chin on the silk parapet.

He lay snoring at my feet but snapped to attention as I headed for the kitchen, his lucky place, where every clatter and clink hints at something edible about to land on the floor. That night it was Parmesan crumbs. I didn't see them fall, only Casey's absorption in licking up every one.

"*Discovering Caravaggio* is off my mother's chair for good," I told Paul. He seemed to think I'd made the right decision.

The Imaginary Poop Patrol

I'd been thinking for a while about taking an improv course. I filed it under "Someday." After Casey made himself at home, I asked myself, "Why not now?" I thought improv had something to do with acting, and I'd done a lot of that in my student days. Hey, I might have talent for this. What we really did in class was play games of transcendent silliness.

Picture some dozen grownups bouncing around the studio, all of us shouting, "Yes, let's!" to various unlikely ideas: Let's blow bubbles, let's play basketball, let's have a pillow fight. There weren't any bubble wands, basketballs or pillows on hand, but that was the whole idea. You had to mime the action, rallying behind your classmate's whim of the moment. You had to make that person look good (the guiding principle of improv), so you held nothing back. You didn't ask yourself, *How am I doing?* or compare your antics to anyone else's. I had to be the oldest person in the room, old enough to be the grandmother of the youngest. When my turn came to lead the tomfoolery, I yelled the first thing that came to mind: "Let's pick up dog poop!"

"Yes, let's!" yelled the group as they stuffed imaginary baggies full of turds. They had no idea what those two words meant to me—the words I'd tried so hard not to say. They didn't know I'd gone dotty for a dog I had to be talked into getting. This game was my chance to exult in dottiness and shower sparks of it on my classmates.

I'd walked to Second City in a fine drizzle that Sunday. I was thinking of someone I loved, a person in trouble. There had to be something I could do besides leave messages this person didn't answer. "You won't always feel like this," I'd say. When I was young, I too had felt Like This and couldn't imagine feeling any other way. I wished my words could plant the seed of a reason to live, which I would sprinkle with a watering can until the sprout pierced its stiff coat and followed the sun above ground. A seedling this tender should not be doused with a hose. A tear slid down my cheek and then another. I wiped them with a wet hand. (My pockets held baggies and treats, not stuff humans need, like tissues.)

I left Second City feeling brighter, more hopeful. I still had a loved one in despair, but I could hold my sadness in one room of my mind and leave the others open to whatever feelings blew in. Amusement at the zaniness that bobbed around our classroom. Astonishment that any wild notion of mine could turn a band of strangers into an imaginary poop patrol. Back home Casey broke into a dance at the sight of me. I didn't kid myself: He was craving dinner, not my company. He teetered on his hind legs and made as if to fly for the kibble as it cascaded into his bowl. Twice a day, the same familiar ecstasy. It never got old, to him or me.

When I was a young working mother at the nadir of my Like This years, a psychiatrist talked some sense into me. She hectored and pontificated but her method proved surprisingly effective. By working with tools I knew, words and ideas, I honed a more constructive way to think about my dilemmas. There followed two rounds of marriage counseling with Annette. I became a firm believer in the power of talking to someone with diplomas on the wall. With Casey I didn't analyze. I simply felt. Like blowing imaginary bubbles while screaming "Yes, let's," it was a whole new way to be. Or should I say a new way to be whole?

Many besides Annette had done their best to guide me to a better way to be. I'd offered up my self-deceptions to that butt-kicking psychiatrist, my tension knots to body workers of various persuasions, my pride to fellow searchers who repeated the Serenity Prayer in a church basement. I chose my mentors based on words, reasons and ideas. Casey reached out to me with paws and nose and tongue. He pulled me into a realm of undiluted feeling. For the first time, I didn't much care what I thought or knew.

Some things about being human can't be learned from your own kind.

Besotted

My first selfie of Casey and me is still the best, and it took some doing. Frame the shot with one hand, offer a treat with the other, keep trying when Casey turned his head at the last second. Ah, finally: Casey in majestic profile, master of all he surveyed from our bench at Corktown Common. Me second fiddle in the background, looking besotted. I posted us to Facebook with a caption from John Donne: "I wonder what thou and I did before we loved." Donne was writing about humans in a rumpled bed, but the sentiment applied just as well to a woman on a bench with her dog—that heart-bursting sense of the world made new, of possibilities undreamed-of in the straitened realm of before.

Lifetimes had passed since I studied "The Good Morrow." In my haste I didn't check the quote, dropped "by my troth" and was promptly caught in the error by a sister poetry geek. If Donne could return from the 17th century, he'd drop it too. I hadn't so much erred as modernized to portray my rapture onscreen where everyone I knew, and some I'd never met, could see it had really happened. There would be a multitude of moments like this one, opening out before me as the grass opened to the pond, the pond to the meadow, the meadow to the floodplain and the trail I walked with Casey. Back home Paul would ask me, "Was he a good boy?" I couldn't answer anything but yes.

I wondered why Annette never asked, "Have you two thought about getting a dog?" With Casey we'd become more kind to each other. The proof was a fight we had, if that's the word. Seasoned partners like us wouldn't lower ourselves to fight over anything as minor as a traffic problem in the kitchen. So let's call it a skirmish. We have a galley kitchen, which matters not at all except when we both have designs on the command post, the central spot within two steps of everything. That morning I was in command, opening the fridge, the dishwasher and any number of cupboards as the spirit moved me, while Paul couldn't make his first cup of coffee of the day without walking into an open door. "Is there a reason," he began, "why you always decide to make lunch just as I'm getting ready for breakfast?"

We only say "Is there a reason . . ." when there can't possibly be a reason. Not one that makes sense, anyway. "Is there a reason . . ." heralds a complaint, not a question. The most annoying reply to all complaints beginning "Is there a reason . . ." is a literal one like mine to Paul that day: "Of course there's a reason. It's time for my lunch. I can't help it if you keep different hours and have just started thinking about breakfast." We were off and bickering. I got to the command post first, he was hungrier.

We didn't notice Casey slink in (where there's a cook, there are crumbs). He caught a whiff of cheese and drooled at my feet, leaving a puddle in which I nearly lost my balance. I yelled, he froze. He hadn't done anything wrong; it's a dog's nature to drool. In the moment I forgot he was a dog and responded as if he were an injured child. "Sorry, Casey."

"Sorry" is a word rarely spoken in our home. I used to think it was only my husband who protected his moral turf in altercations, when the truth is we both did. I wanted to hear "sorry," not to say it myself. After a great many years, I realized that what matters isn't saying "sorry," but being more kind in the future. By the time I slipped in Casey's drool, I had finally figured this out but I was overdue for a refresher. Because "sorry" means nothing to Casey, it opened a space in which I could imagine being as considerate to my husband as I am to our dog. Hungry humans tend to get peevish without at least a cup of coffee; it's their nature. Inspired by the drool incident, I began to ask Paul when he might want the run of the kitchen. From then on we had one less reason to confront each other with indefensible annoyances.

Casey excelled at neutralizing irritation. It had something to do with his repertoire of cheerful sounds, all variants on "Here I am." His tags jingled like Christmas bells, his paws raked the dog bed to make it soft. Before a walk he whinnied with excitement (but only if Paul was the walker). He didn't lap his water like the feline Casey Jones. He had the most explosive slurp. I took to calling, "Hey, Casey! Think you could slurp a little louder?"

In my magazine days, I presided over stories on how to warm a home with weekend decor projects. Personally, I never had time to get creative with paper and paint, or shop for new throws in seasonal colors. With a dog in residence, there wasn't any need to warm the place. Casey took care of that on his daily rounds, following the slant of light and the currents of the air to the spot that suited him best. I never knew how many sweet spots we had until he made them his, at least one in every room.

Our home had never looked so welcoming—or so furry. Our pants weren't the half of it. Casey released a haze of fluff, which turned up in the strangest places. Stovetop, bathroom vanity, computer keyboard, even inside books and running shoes. It floated on the air like dust motes, tumbleweeded in corners. While stirring a bean stew, I found a single ginger hair nestled under a rosemary sprig. Nothing in our home was truly ours anymore without a fleck or two of ginger fur.

The best part of having a dog, according to every dog person I know, is the unconditional love. They mean the dog's. I found it was the love he released in me to shower upon random strangers. Muralist atop his ladder: "I love what you're doing!" Groundskeeper pruning trees in a park: "Thank you for the work you do." Dog walker whose perky brown mini-poo lay down in the sidewalk until I led Casey past: "This must be the famous Archie!"

The muralist and the groundskeeper waved. The dog walker snapped, "This is Coco!" I'd heard tell of an endearing mini-poo, apparently a ringer for Coco, whose defining trait was a prostration habit. In my eagerness to befriend the famous Archie, I seemed to have crossed a social boundary.

I didn't think I was capable of being overly familiar. As a child afraid of talking to strangers, I once refused a ride home from school in a torrential rainstorm with a mom who had room for one more in her station wagon full of kids. She told my mother, who laughed at my literal-mindedness. How it would amuse her to know I'd intruded on someone's private moment with his mini-poo.

I was starting to see that a dog is more than the canine animal. A dog is everywhere you go together, every living creature you meet along the way, and the human you become with your canine.

Any halfway observant acquaintance could see the fountain overflow. I'd just set out my mat for Pilates when I felt Sharon's gaze. She was teaching that day for the first time in months, and I thought perhaps I'd put on weight—until she said, with a sisterly grin, "Rona, you look radiant! Are you in love?"

No one had ever asked me, "Are you in love?" And now that someone had—someone whose usual focus is the firing (or not) of my glutes—I realized love was spilling out of me, the sing-his-name, can't-keep-my hands-off-him kind, bouncy as the Beatles in the madcap days of "Yeah, yeah, yeah." I thought I'd found a new note on the emotional scale, a new color on the spectrum, and I couldn't keep this burst of yeah-yeah-yeahness to myself. "We've adopted a dog. He's changed our lives."

My classmates humored me, as dog people do when a first-timer joins their ranks. If they didn't currently have a dog, they remembered dogs gone by. They already knew Casey's story, but instead of changing the subject, they encouraged me to babble on for Sharon. Listening to each other was part of our deal. In Pilates you could kvell about your first grandchild, vent about your crazy-making relatives, recount the details of your photo op with the stars of *Outlander*. So why not sing the praises, one more time, of a jailbird dog named for a cat?

I was just getting into the details of Casey's life so far. I could have gone on but Pilates breathing made it hard to talk. In, in, out, out. CaSEY, CaSEY. I breathed his name.

Part II: Belonging

One of Us

When Paul said, "Let's get a dog," my number one objection wasn't any of the quibbles I raised that night. If I had it in me to love a dog, then I surely would have loved the Maynard family's Nicky. He was smart, frisky, gentle with children. A fine dog, according to everyone but me.

I spurned him.

Nicky just happened, the way things did in our family. I still wonder why. My father might have said to my mother, "Let's get a dog." He was the one with the soft spot for animals, especially dogs, but Nicky could just as well have been my mother's idea. She only tolerated animals, but anything to distract her husband from drinking. I was about 15, Joyce four years younger. We hadn't asked for a dog when we learned that a puppy was coming to Maynard Hall. This puppy couldn't possibly be about us.

The one story my father told about his childhood, and retold time and again, involved a dog. On the ship that took his family from England to Canada, he met a pretty and ebullient young woman who traveled with her pup. She had noticed the sketchbook young Max Maynard carried everywhere. Could he please draw a picture of her dog? Max couldn't have been more than ten, but he already liked pretty women as much as he liked dogs. He meant to impress and did. "You will be an artist!" she exclaimed.

We never knew what kind of dog he had captured with his pencil, and in his eyes it didn't matter. To him the dog was not a dog, but a destiny unfulfilled. After a promising start as a painter, he parlayed a bachelor's degree into a perennial assistant professorship at the University of New Hampshire, where he taught 18th-century literature and became a campus legend for drawing on the blackboard as he lectured. In a few flowing lines he could conjure William Blake's tiger. This was as close as he had come to artistic renown. His gallery was Maynard Hall, but nothing he hung there pleased him for long. He would rip paintings off the walls and spirit them away to his attic studio, where he pursued his calling after hours. It was frigid in the winter, suffocatingly hot in summer. While making and unmaking art, my father drank. A painting might die in a fury of corrective measures.

The coming of the puppy was announced at the teak dining room table that I always brushed before dinner with a miniature brass broom. Surrounding us, paintings that measured up, for now. "A brilliant, original man," my mother used to say, her excuse for his tirades and other shameful eccentricities—dusty stacks of exams he never got around to marking, fights he picked with colleagues at faculty parties.

Any dog of ours could only be brilliant and original. The dogs of Durham, New Hampshire, were mostly Labs, mutts and German shepherds. My parents decided that we would have a standard poodle, a breed noted for intelligence. He'd cut a dashing figure with his pompom tail and crowning pouf of curls.

I didn't dare want this puppy. I lived by an unspoken rule: Wanting sets you up for disappointment. Ever since I could remember, my father had tainted everything. Picnics at the beach (we'd no sooner unpacked the egg salad than he'd mutter about getting home for tea). Trimming the tree (always pronounced our most beautiful yet, but never beautiful enough to keep away the gloom that ambushed my father every Christmas). Whatever happened or did not at Maynard Hall, his moods drove it and had the power to spoil it. We never said "alcoholic," except of skid-row bums and Richard Burton, yet we lived in thrall to one. I burned with resentment.

In spite of myself, I did want the puppy. I wanted the lightness of spirit that he promised, the freedom not to worry about triggering an outburst or falling short of the family standards. My father held forth in complete paragraphs about art and life; my mother had a doctorate from Radcliffe and a penchant for quoting Tennyson or Milton at the dinner table. My sister and I won national writing contests, both of us intent on Projects. We Maynards looked down on those who didn't have our taste, our accomplishments, but I could never figure out if we were better than everyone else, or not as good and pretending otherwise. A

Maynard could not be a child among children, a neighbor among neighbors.

I envied people who didn't have to justify their existence. It seemed to me they all had dogs.

Normal families tooled around in station wagons with dogs leaning out rolled-down windows. Those people went places we didn't—Fenway Park, the White Mountains. By my teens, I'd lost interest in seeing those places. I preferred to stay in my room, playing ballads of doomed love on my guitar. But the day we collected our puppy, I had to witness the excitement. That part wasn't just another wild hope. It happened. We piled into our Studebaker Lark, the only new car we ever owned, and brought home the most bewitching creature. He thrust his nose out the window, silky black ears flying as he inhaled the world. He reminded me of Scuppers on the prow of his ship, setting out for a great adventure. In his presence the Lark seemed bound for somewhere more thrilling than Maynard Hall and its inviolable routines.

My father must have loosened his customary two-handed grip on the wheel. Sober, he had a gift for joy. We laughed all the way home.

The family meeting to name our puppy might have been the only one we ever had. I wanted to call him Dylan, a homage to two of my heroes: the young firebrand of "Blowin' in the Wind," and the wild-hearted Welshman of "Do Not Go Gentle into That Good Night." The family vetoed Dylan. I could have seen the case for Boswell, after Samuel Johnson's biographer, or Mozart, whose horn concertos played while my mother passed canapes to guests. But for the first time in memory, my family went middlebrow. They wanted something catchy and easy to call, a name with some pep. Joyce, our resident expert on pep, came up with Nicky and carried the day.

If I could weigh in today, I too would take Nicky over Dylan. The canine ear, it's said, responds best to names with hard consonants and long vowels, in particular a peppy final "e." But by not becoming Dylan, Nicky proved I was the misfit in my family (it's not as if I fitted in anywhere else). That was the first thing I held against him.

Nicky didn't stay bewitching for long. When my parents chose a poodle, they overlooked the cost of grooming and the drive out of town to get it done. Clumps of hair obscured Nicky's eyes. He smelled of brackish ponds (and every so often a skunk). His blithe dishevelment embarrassed me. I can still see the two of us together, if together is the word for two beings as uncomfortably bonded as we were.

I'm walking to Oyster River High School with my arms full of books and my gaze straight ahead lest anyone suspect the galoot cavorting at my heels—a stick in his mouth, burrs in his tail—has anything to do with me. I pretend Nicky doesn't exist, but he's too enthused to get the message. And too loyal. As a Maynard, I am his and have no say in the matter. I can't lose him, try as I might. That's the second thing I held against Nicky.

Nicky knew from the start whose dog he really was. My father's mood swung high and low, the highs pure happiness for Nicky. I picture them heading out on a country walk, Nicky with his shaggy head uplifted and the bounce of comradeship in his step, the dog mirroring the human with the sketchbook under his arm. My father strikes the gravel with a shiny walking stick from the collection he keeps by the door. Stride, stride, thump. The rhythm track to a song only he and Nicky can hear.

I see the two adventurers back home, my father leafing through the latest *New Yorker*. My mother has wheeled away the teacart; the scent of roast capon wafts from the kitchen. A fire crackles, set by my father according to his protocol. In his hand, a glass of beer. Nicky sprawls at his feet, eyes hidden by that thicket of curls. "Hmm-hmm," says my father, his voice falling on the second "hmm" as if the magazine confirms what he knows to be at hand—the collapse of all things beautiful and good. Nicky lifts his head; he alone can speak his master's wordless language of dejection. He answers with a grunt of sympathy. "Poor old Nicky," says my father. "Nobody cares about you."

Did he ever say, "Good boy"?

Only Joyce treated Nicky like a loved and lovable dog, not an alter-ego or a nuisance. She watched *The Andy Griffith Show* with her arm draped around his neck, rode her Schwinn bike while he trotted beside her. It wasn't enough. Melancholy settled on Nicky. When he was in, he wanted to be out. No sooner out, he'd whimper to come in. He paced the finish off the floorboards in front of our door.

Back then I didn't acknowledge that animals have emotions. "Dumb animals," I called them. I couldn't see how a dog both absorbs and reflects the emotional climate of a home. When humans look the other way, the dog is a steadfast witness to the truth. Nicky came to us a buoyant adventurer, but he didn't lead the Maynards to a brave new world. It was the other way around: We pulled him into our misery.

I longed to be part of some other family. My ingratitude for the family I had was a scab I picked bloody. That was the third, hardest thing I held against Nicky.

After my mother threw my father out, he sought refuge for a while in the Sussex countryside. Nicky wandered around Maynard Hall like a page without a lord. He perked up when I brought my toddler home to New Hampshire, thinking I too was done with marriage. Our house had never felt so cheerful. It rang with shouts and squeals, punctuated with the banging of stainless-steel pots that had found a new purpose as Ben's favorite toys. Nicky would observe this game as if his services might be required. When Ben struck him in the head with a flying lid (and chortled at landing the blow), Nicky didn't flinch.

"You mustn't hurt Nicky," I said, meaning to teach Ben kindness. I didn't know then what can happen when a child hurts a dog. To some dogs, a well-aimed lid might be a biting offense. But Nicky seemed to understand that Ben was driven by mischief, not malice. He intuited the moods of other species. I still didn't have a clue.

I once let Nicky tag along on an outing to the barns where the university's agriculture department housed its livestock. Open to the public without supervision, the barns brought Old MacDonald's farm to life. My father used to take me there, holding my hand as I marveled at the animals—the size of their hoofs and haunches, the bright abundance of their pee. Hay and ripe manure made my nose tingle. Now it was my turn to share this magic place with my child.

I parked the stroller not far from a cluster of grazing cattle. "Cow! Cow!" shrieked Ben. What was the harm in a closer look? I set him free to stagger toward the cattle. Nicky stiffened and began to growl. "Oh, Nicky," I muttered. "What's got into you? They're only cows."

Ben had just about reached them, waving his arms. A deep rumble arose from the cows. Not the gentle lowing of "Away in a Manger," but something ominous, an earthquake sound. The cows weren't chewing their cud anymore. They had massed themselves, a phalanx of muscle and hooves closing in on my son.

I flew to Ben, scooped him into my arms. Nicky may have bared his teeth to intimidate the cows. He may have created some kind of distraction. Whatever he did as I ran, it was the right thing to do. I never told anyone how terrified I was for my child. How ashamed that Nicky warned me, and I refused to listen.

I went back to Paul. My father came back to New Hampshire and made a home with Nicky. Two disappointed geezers they were—both arthritic, Nicky with a missing toe. I shrugged off the news that my father had put him down. Nothing sad about that, I told myself. He'd lived a respectable span.

Years later, I fell in love with Casey and found myself thinking of my first good boy—for that he was, although I couldn't see it at the time. I wondered what my father said to Nicky at the end, hoped it wasn't "Poor old Nicky." My father was not a weeping man. He carried himself like a warrior whose enemy was fate—shoulders back, square jaw forward. Anger stiffened him; grief didn't seem to crack him, but I think he must have wept for Nicky.

There aren't many people left who remember Nicky. In family albums he's a dark blur, an accidental presence viewed from behind or far away. His puppyhood slipped by without a single photo. I looked for his name in the files my mother left of her voluminous letters, typed single-space and carbon-copied for posterity. Among all the stories she told about people who amused, intrigued or enraged her, there had to be a story or two about Nicky. What a tale she could have spun about bringing him home ("You won't believe it. I can hardly believe it myself, but we've found the most bewitching puppy"). I guess that story didn't interest her. From her letters, you'd think we never had a silky-eared puppy who leaned out the window of the Lark as if he were poised to fly. But we did, we did. I stroked his ears. I felt the surge of elation. Then I felt it slip away.

An Etiquette Lesson

I'd never much cared for snow, but Casey had many ways to love it. Bury his snout in it, tracking who knew what. Sign it with his pee. Lick it, sniff it, crunch it, kick it up. New snow meant fun for Casey, which made it fun for me.

Early one Sunday I looked out at freshly snow-covered rooftops and decided to seize the moment. While other dog walkers were still checking Facebook in their bathrobes, Casey and I could make the first footprints at the dog park. The temperature had plunged overnight, but I knew how to dress for outings like this one. Cashmere pants over leggings. Ankle-length coat, 20 years old and stained with salt at the hem, but a winter dog walker's best friend. Fleece hat pulled down to my eyebrows. Matted, fake-fur gloves that made my hands look like paws but kept them warm. Who would see me? Only Casey, no stickler for fashion. He'd already sprayed pee on the underside of his new turtleneck sweater.

We had the dog park to ourselves, white and glistening. Up and down Casey tore amid puffs of snow. At rest he was not the most gracefully proportioned dog, his legs too short for his brawny trunk, but at a gallop he became a streak of power and purpose. Drizzles of yellow appeared here and there, each one a signal to his own kind: *I was here first. Show some respect.* The snow was less deep than I hoped, and Casey's flying paws exposed patches of frozen brown earth. But we hadn't come for the aesthetics.

I reached into my pocket for the well-chewed, urine-yellow tennis ball that looked like every other ball abandoned in dog parks, although ours had a history that made it special. Our ball once belonged to Heather and her sheepdog mix, Melvin, who took a shine to Casey in this very park. We'd arrived without a ball of our own, so Heather lent me one of theirs, with M written on it in black Magic Marker. "Keep it," she said as they left. I rolled the mottled ball in my palm. Chewed, muddied, cracked and slobbered upon, it looked almost ready for the trash but it had been a talisman for Heather. Melvin was her father's name. A heart attack took him just before she got the dog.

I threw our tennis ball for Casey, my usual under-handed bobble. He carried it away for a vigorous licking. He couldn't get the hang of fetch, so all the fetching in this game fell to me. Toss the ball, trudge after Casey to retrieve it. Over and over, the same klutzy, back-straining shuffle. At least there was no one in the park to snicker at my ineptitude.

Behind me I heard a soft click, someone opening the gate. I hoped it was Heather. Casey hadn't played with Melvin in ages. No, a young man had joined us with a shapely hound. A ball arced and spun as the man threw it. "Hey, Molly!" Off went the dog, as fleet as she was elegant. She knew her stuff, this dog. Casey, who did not, ran after her, madly yapping. Too fast for him, she nabbed the ball on the fly and dropped it, bowing, at her human's feet. A red ball, new and shiny. Casey stole it and took off. Molly's human pursed his lips. *Bad move, Casey.*

I hadn't spent much time in dog parks, but I knew the etiquette around balls: Bring your own in case your dog makes off with someone else's. The Heathers of the world don't mind, but this guy was another breed. I yelled Casey's name, waved the tennis ball and launched it in what proved to be the wrong direction. "He's not very smart," I said, too brightly. "He thinks he's got room in his mouth for two balls. You'll see."

Heather had found this amusing. *Dogs! So goofy and we love them for it.* This fellow didn't crack a smile. Underdressed for the weather in layers of black and gray that looked freshly dry-cleaned, he stiffened as Molly brought him our tennis ball, mottled by the drool of many tongues. He didn't seem to like such an object sullying his glove, but Molly was wagging her tail. He threw. She ran. Casey chased her, barking all the way. "That's not normal," said the man in black and gray. "That dog of yours has no manners."

I stumbled after Casey, leash in hand. My heavy coat flapped around my ankles; my bootlaces dragged in the snow. "Casey! Drop it!" I might as well have asked him to mix me a Negroni. Whichever ball Molly had in her possession, Casey wanted it. The faster she outran him, the louder he barked. Molly was a seasoned dog, too poised to be rattled by a pesky whippersnapper like Casey. I liked Molly, which is more than I could say for her human. Still, I didn't foresee what came over the man. He seethed, he spat, he trembled. Time fell away as he vented for what seemed like many minutes but was probably one or two. Language all but dwindled to the single word that he aimed, like a hammer against a skull, at my dog and me.

When this word appeared in the magazine I edited—rarely, always in dialog, and printed in full because I loathed the coy "f____," I could count on a flurry of cancellations. I like the bluntness of a single, considered "fuck" between friends but try not to indulge with anyone I don't know well. It has an unpredictable power to dismay, especially coming from a woman of my generation. For me to speak this word—in some circles, anyway—is to shout, fart and flash, all at once. Not even my father, entitled to rage by his manhood, said anything close to fuck. My father's idea of profanity was an archaic Britishism, "Ah, lud."

I could dodge the whole meltdown by leaving the room. But until I caught Casey, who was tearing after Molly, I'd be stuck in the dog park. Taking Mr. F-Bomb's verbal bludgeoning.

His weapon of choice has many variations: the -er, the -ing, the -head, the -up and the -wit, the sick one and the dumb one. He must have let fly with most. It's hard to keep tabs when you are in a state of shock, but I got the gist. I'd better train my abnormal fucking dog. I should wise up and get a book but selfish fucks like me thought we could let our fucking dogs do whatever the fuck they want.

In his rank patois I detected primal roots, as if Casey

and I were stand-ins for every driver who'd cut him off in traffic, every waiter who served him a burger not cooked to his standards, every date who'd given him the brush-off. Coaches who benched him, classmates who didn't invite him to their birthday parties. The know-nothing kid sister—or was it a golden big brother—who got all the breaks from Mom and Dad. He and Molly had both balls now—one in a mouth, the other in a glove, but this was not about Molly anymore.

He consumed my entire field of vision, all angles from the jut of the hem on his jacket to the set of his jaw. I had his number, yet he cowed me. Shamed me too, for letting myself be silenced by a furious overgrown toddler who could speak barely more than one word, yet presumed to be the arbiter of normal behavior. And Mr. F-Bomb wasn't done with me. Sneering, he delivered his final flourish: "Nobody ever told you the truth before, did they?"

He looked young enough to be the second child I never had, the last-chance baby conceived on the cusp of menopause. Would he talk to his mother like this? Perhaps he saved his worst outbursts for her. Maybe he lived in his mother's basement and gave her hell for not stocking the fridge with the only acceptable brew. Some would have said, "Hey, buddy. You want to talk about my dog's manners, how about you watch your own and dial back the language?"

I dredged up a few words, as if from the bottom of a well: "You're being a prick." Ms. Nice Girl. How cringingly evasive. "Being a prick" means momentarily acting like one, as opposed to embodying prickishness. And "prick" fell short of what the situation demanded. Casey had been a prick, a nuisance rather than a threat, off gallivanting while Mr. F-Bomb cursed us both. Mr. F-Bomb was a bully. While we glowered at each other, hands in our pockets, a white car pulled up outside the park. On its side a blue band: Parking Enforcement. Mr. F-Bomb sprinted to the gate with Molly at his heels: "Please don't tow me! I'm about to move!" He sounded like a child in trouble, his voice high and frantic.

With Molly gone, Casey had no one to impress. He bounded to my side and waited for me to loop his leash around my waist. Mr. F-Bomb would have mocked that leash. Hands-free, the sure sign of a fucking idiot who can't control a dog. It needed an adjustment impossible to manage in my paw-like gloves, but when I took them off, I ran into a different problem: numb fingers. I craved a warm blanket and a cup of hot cider. Fumbled with the grommets on the leash but it still wasn't right. Bent to tie my boots but the laces slipped from my fingers. Casey looked up at me, switching his tail, as if he couldn't understand how long this was taking. *That makes two of us, Casey.*

Correction: four of us. Mr. F-Bomb hadn't moved his car. Despite what he promised the parking enforcement officer, who'd moved on in search of other targets, he was sitting inside it with Molly. Waiting for us to move on so the trampled park could be theirs. But I couldn't seem to get my act together. Was it the cold that stilled my fingers or the ignominy of being watched by the F-bomber? Behind him I could make out Molly's regal profile.

All the way home I wondered how such a sorry excuse for a human could have a dog like Molly in his corner. I'd met plenty of other bullies, but he was the first to target Casey. Casey had softened me, yet this man remained hard and self-righteous despite Molly's devotion. In a final indignity, he still had the chewed-up ball Heather had given me as one dog person to another. He'd probably toss it in the garbage without pausing to wonder who M was. I looked down at Casey, who was spraying the pockmarked corner of a building. *I was here first. Show some respect.* That's the spirit, Casey.

We found Paul watching soccer with his first latte of the day. He muted the game to hear my story. "You should have called 911," he said.

"I was flustered. My mind went blank."

Sunlight glinted on snow outside our window. A spray of flowers Paul had brought me overflowed the vase— asters, sea lavenders and baby's breath. He always asked for no yellow, my color of last resort, and the florist had outdone himself with shades of indigo and violet. Things looked exactly as they should on Sunday morning, but I kept seeing Mr. F-Bomb.

I admitted to myself what I couldn't in the dog park, how physically vulnerable I'd been, within striking distance of a man electrified by rage. If I'd called 911, he might have made a run for me and no one was around to stop him. Casey would have defended me, but Molly, loyal dog that she was, would tear into us both. Mr. F-Bomb deserved a blast of his own word of choice in all its variety: the -er, the -ing, the -head. The -up and the -wit, the sick one and the dumb one.

There's nothing like a good dinner to redeem a bad day. Casey curled up in his accustomed spot while the scent of roasted garlic wafted from our plates. The rampage at the dog park was still on my mind but my perspective had shifted. "He needs that dog," I told Paul. "She must be the best relationship he's got. Maybe the only one that's not a mess. And you know what?" I didn't know myself, not fully, until I spoke the words. "He must have at least something to do with why she's a special dog. A touch, a tone of voice. And maybe she draws something out of him that humans can't reach."

We had that in common, he and I. Casey was having the same effect on me.

Dog with a Past

The man on my mind had been in serious trouble. He'd gone to prison, where he trained a ginger puppy who loved him. "Down," he said, and down went the pup who would be ours. Not the first time, maybe not the 21st. Casey's not the fastest learner, but a good trainer has patience. The prisoner was good. Months after leaving his care, Casey still dropped to his haunches when Laurie said "Down." He never did for us, and we lost interest in trying. We had nothing to prove by commanding a dog to lie down, but the prisoner did. A prisoner with a gift for training dogs will have a warm friend in a cold place and a potential career path outside. Before we loved our dog, this man did. Our benefactor.

When I realized that Paul was the One, no detail of his past was beneath my notice. Former girlfriends intrigued me most of all because it was with them that he learned to love. He used to tell a story of the high school sweetheart who went out on a drive with her family and failed to call at the appointed hour. Fearing a terrible accident, he rang and rang her house. Paul could tell me who he was before we loved. With Casey I had to guess.

If not for his first love, Casey wouldn't be Casey. But of course he wasn't Casey then, several names ago. We both wondered what the Benefactor used to call him. Not Tucker, his name on the rescue site. Or Shotgun, his shelter name. In a prison you surely don't name a dog for a weapon. He must have had some other name, forgotten by everyone but the Benefactor and himself. "Someday we'll take him to a dog park, and someone will yell his prison name," I mused. "He'll come running. That's how we'll know." It never seemed all that likely, but there had to be something we could learn about Casey's first love. And the name he called Casey seemed to me like a good tidbit.

I started reading up on prison dog-training programs. Some prepare cast-off dogs to be family pets, others to be service animals. These programs nurture love and then they cut it short. In, out, next. I found a video online of an inmate saying goodbye to a severely abused black Lab who had blossomed in his care. Young enough to have a hint of baby fat still in his cheeks, the man looks like someone you'd meet at the playground, catching his preschooler at the bottom of the slide. He has trained lots of dogs in prison and keeps a photo of almost every one, but he's never loved a dog like Esther. Today a van will carry her away to a new home. "She didn't want to go," he says after their parting embrace. "I'm really going to miss her." I know his first name: Jason.

That's more than I knew about the man who trained Casey. Prison veteran or young first offender? Family waiting for him or no one at all? He'll spend the rest of his life with a prison record. There ought to be another kind of record, the stories of dogs he trained and families who gave them a real home, with no bars or body searches. Had anyone bothered to thank him?

I Googled the warden of Belmont Correctional Institution in St. Clairsville, Ohio. Her kind face gave me hope. What a brutal job she must have. So much flak from prisoners, activists, the union, old-school guards who resented working for a woman. I could write the email that would make her day and might help me get through to the Benefactor.

Dear Warden,

My husband and I are the lucky adopters of a young adult rescue dog who spent his puppyhood in your prison.

Between leaving the prison and arriving in our home, Casey spent 11 weeks in your local shelter. Yet he came to us happy, affectionate, aware of some basic commands and eager to learn more. We predict he'll make friends wherever he goes.

I hope you'll convey our gratitude to the person or people responsible.

Best regards,

Rona Maynard

I embedded the photo of Casey and Paul being guys together. While I wasn't counting on a photo of the Benefactor, it didn't seem impossible.

The warden replied within hours. Wonderful news, love the photo. So glad to hear the program sent us a happy dog. We should keep loving our good boy. That was the gist of it, minus the triple-exclamation marks. No indication of any word of thanks passed on. I should have known the warden didn't run an interspecies social club. With luck the Benefactor would be out by now, earning a living as a dog trainer. Coming home to a forever dog of his own. If I had a photo of this man, I'd pin it to my bulletin board so I could see his face from my desk. But the closest thing I had to an image was the grainy shape in my mind—neither short nor tall, stocky nor thin, barely adult nor almost senior.

At least I could picture Casey's old stomping ground. Okay, Google. Show me St. Clairsville, Ohio.

All I meant to do was form a picture of the place. It didn't look like our kind of destination. While Paul and I have road-tripped our way through plenty of tucked-away hamlets, we expect at least a hint of local character (a famous pit master would do nicely). St. Clairsville came up short. It does have Ohio's only rail trail with a tunnel, but we're not cyclists. It's got the Ohio Valley Mall, TripAdvisor's choice for number one local attraction, but reviewers were put off by all the empty storefronts. It boasts a profusion of flowers and trees, for which it won an America in Bloom Award some years ago. The mayor's promotional video informed me that "anyone who has lived in a small town wants to come back to a small town." Everyone smiled in the video, and every face was white. The town is the county seat of Belmont County, which Donald Trump had recently carried with nearly 70 percent of the vote. If we ever went to St. Clairsville, a ridiculous thought, we'd be wise not to speak of politics or religion.

Sometimes I imagined what Casey would be doing in St. Clairsville, if anyone there had wanted him. He'd be riding around in a pickup truck with an NRA bumper sticker. His best pal, a hunter in a MAGA cap, would know what to do with the dog then known as Shotgun—set him loose to bay and point, then reward him for a job well done.

The two could have stepped from the folk song "Old Blue," in which the hunter roasts freshly killed possum with a couple of sweet potatoes and shares the meal with his loyal hound. "Old Blue" didn't touch me before we had Casey, but lately I'd been searching YouTube for the most soulful version. The Byrds sounded too perky, Joan Baez too self-consciously plangent. The only one I could picture as a hunter in the Mississippi Valley, grieving the best friend he had, was raspy-voiced Dave Van Ronk. When Van Ronk lowers Blue into his grave with a golden chain, you can hear the world cracking.

The people of St. Clairsville would have present-day versions of Blue. I thought it must be one of those places where gun shops outnumber restaurants that are still serving lunch at three (road-tripping through North Carolina, we'd gone hungry in such a town). But according to the website of the local chamber of commerce, St. Clairsville has as many gun shops as bookstores. Zero. Around about my third virtual tour of the place, I began to daydream about taking Casey back.

Paul didn't exactly say, "Let's go to St. Clairsville"—although if he had, I'd have thought he was reading my mind. I didn't think of myself as the kind of person who travels to her dog's hometown, but Paul gave me cover. As he positioned the trip, it wasn't about St. Clairsville. We are both the kind of people who would travel to Fallingwater, the celebrated house Frank Lloyd Wright designed to crown a waterfall in the woods of southwestern Pennsylvania. Wright's masterpiece and Casey's hometown could be part of the same three-day jaunt. Paul had the itinerary all figured out, the two stops within easy drives of a dog-friendly Hampton Inn on the outskirts of Pittsburgh. It met our new standards of hotel nirvana: instead of a destination restaurant and five stars on TripAdvisor, no pet fees and Camp Bow Wow practically at the front door. While we feasted on beauty at "the house of the century" (as Wright's masterpiece was described by none other than his rival, Philip Johnson), Casey would be having too much fun to miss us.

We'd been talking for years about a trip to Fallingwater. Nearly got there once, then returned it to the Someday file. Why not now?

The travel mavens of Pilates liked to talk about where we were going next. Someone always had a tip to share. Tokyo: Have you booked a spot at Jiro's sushi bar? Oslo: Don't miss the world's largest sculpture park. I could have said, "We're on our way to Fallingwater," but I skipped the cover story. The studio went silent at my news. Camden, Maine, or Santa Barbara, California, might have piqued respectful curiosity, if not a suggestion for dinner. St. Clairsville, Ohio, did not. These women had indulged me through story after story about Casey, but I'd just crossed the line between love and losing it. A classmate said, stifling laughter, "You're going to your dog's hometown?"

Millions of people from all over the world have made the pilgrimage to Fallingwater. Who puts St. Clairsville at the top of a bucket list? People bonkers about their St. Clairsville mutt, and proud of it. I couldn't wait.

A Canine Roots Tour

S mall towns like to proclaim their uniqueness to the world. There's Corbin, Kentucky, the birthplace of Colonel Sanders's secret recipe. South Williamsport, Pennsylvania, home of the Little League Baseball World Series. Riverside, Iowa, the future birthplace of Captain James T. Kirk. A town we drove through and promptly forgot announced itself as the birthplace of a basketball coach whose name we couldn't make out. As we pulled into St. Clairsville, Paul noted the absence of a sign saying, "Birthplace of Casey Jones, Arch-Enemy of Rodents."

This was not the first roots tour for Paul and me. On a family trip more than 30 years ago, we drove into the Dorset Village of Sherborne, where Paul had lived as a child and both his aunts still did. I'd heard plenty about the charms of Sherborne—its medieval abbey, its half-timbered buildings, its "new" castle built by Sir Walter Raleigh (the old one, a ruin, dated back to the 12th century). I might have shown some respect for this journey, but I had my

Walkman on and Bruce Springsteen raising hell in my ears. Halfway into Sherborne, Paul got annoyed. Couldn't I turn off the music for his return to Sherborne? Things were different in St. Clairsville. Casey didn't give a squirrel's ass for human ceremony.

From the road, we couldn't see the Belmont County Animal Shelter. I thought we were lost until someone gave us a tip: "Hang a left at the building that looks like a haunted house. Keep going into the trees." No exaggeration about that building—Mrs. Rochester should have lived in the attic. You couldn't design a more baleful-looking gatehouse for a high-kill shelter. Around the bend, a canine chorus told us we'd arrived. The place resembled the weather-beaten home of a free spirit who doesn't mind pee stains on the carpet. In a shady pen outside, the dogs had plenty of room to stretch their legs. We'd agreed that I would check out the shelter while Paul waited in the car with Casey, sparing him from trauma. As Liz told it, he'd nearly met his doom inside its doors.

The woman at the front desk looked friendly. She could have been the waitress who remembers how you like your eggs, the checkout clerk who always asks about your family. If you lived next door and ran into any kind of trouble, she'd bring the same noodle casserole her mother used to make for these moments. I told her what I knew of Casey's past: the prison, her shelter, the journey to Canada. "I've come from Toronto to say thank you for looking after him when he was homeless. He's a great dog and you must have something to do with that. We thought you could help us fill in some gaps in his story."

She didn't seem impressed that I'd come all the way from Toronto. I got the feeling that to her each adoption was a landmark, one as worthy as another. Could I describe Casey?

I whipped out my phone. "Just a minute. I'll show you a photo." It took a lot more than a minute to unearth a photo of Casey. What was the passcode to the file where I kept all my photos? A tsunami of emotion had washed it away. My fingers froze on the screen. I rang Paul in the car and begged for help. He jokingly calls himself my tech consultant but that morning he saw no humor in the role. "I'm supposed to remember this stuff? It's your account, not mine."

The woman took a call. Kittens clawed at their cage. A door swung open behind me as the missing passcode finally came to mind. Up came a photo of Casey nestled on his bed. I was proud of that shot, in which his almond eyes looked particularly knowing. If any shot of mine would make a stranger in St. Clairsville exclaim at his beauty, that would be the one. Without a smile or a second's hesitation, she said, "I recognize this dog." It had been three and a half years, and God knows how many dogs.

In the doorway stood a woman with disheveled hair, as if she'd come straight from the shower. "I'm the one who called about a donation. We've lost our two greyhounds. They had a lot of stuff we thought you could use." She'd brought both her parents, hollow-eyed, and a couple of crestfallen kids. I told the family I was sorry for their loss.

The old man carried a hamper full of crumpled bags of dog food. Maybe he wasn't all that old, but sorrow was having its way with him. He let out a long sigh. "The second dog died of grief for the first one."

I didn't hear the desk clerk summon two work-booted helpers from the back. But there they stood like ushers at a funeral, heads lowered. A moment of silence passed before they held out their arms for the dog food.

The family had many more hampers to unload. While they worked, the desk clerk told me what she knew about Casey. From the shelter, his first stop, he went to the prison. After basic training, he returned to the shelter for adoption as a family pet. One thing still puzzled me. How did Casey ever get to Canada? The woman at the desk couldn't say. The colleague who arranged that transfer was no longer at the shelter, and they'd never again sent dogs north of the border. There simply wasn't any need.

"We were told this is a high-kill shelter," I said.

The desk clerk's eyes widened. "Oh, no! This is a no-kill shelter!"

We didn't need any help finding Belmont Correctional Institution, which sits at the bottom of a winding road bordered by swaths of green. It resembled the approach to a municipal golf course until we saw the barbed wire and the distant figures performing chores involving large sacks. Gray shirts, dark pants. If I'd taken a photo, it wouldn't have looked like much. And I'd have made myself an object of suspicion.

You don't just drop in at a prison, taking souvenir shots as you go. What was I expecting we'd do here? Present ourselves with Casey's most adorable photo in the hope that some armed guard in a metal booth would say, "I recognize this dog"?

A woman strode toward us with a small tight smile and a prominent badge. Paul rolled down the window as if a cop had pulled him over. She asked, "May I help you?" She meant, "Do you people have business here?" Behind her loomed the entrance, a bland gray box off limits to tourists on a canine roots trip.

"Our dog came from this prison. One of your prisoners did a great job with his training. We'd like to say thanks." Casey had just poked his head out the window for a sniff—and a treat, if the woman had any in her pocket.

Instead he got a smile, a real one this time. "They do a wonderful job with the dogs. I adopted one myself. Beagle. Best dog in the world."

"Second best," Paul said. The woman flinched. It took her a minute to realize he wasn't insulting her beagle, he was just devoted to his own.

Time to move on. Nothing to see. But somewhere on the grounds or inside, prisoners and dogs were at work together. Maybe the Benefactor was still among them. He'd never know we'd driven from Toronto in his honor.

Everywhere we travel, we're drawn to realtors' windows. We've shuddered at poky London flats that could be ours in exchange for everything we own. We've marveled at estates we could afford—trout stream, guest suite, the works—on the outskirts of Nowheresville. As we see it, the way to get a feel for a place is to picture yourself living there. In

St. Clairsville we skipped this exercise. We'd come to picture Casey's past, not imaginary futures for ourselves. After lunch we'd be done with this town.

When you travel with a dog, you get used to eating your lunch outside. You can do a lot worse than a wrought iron table in downtown St. Clairsville on a Thursday afternoon in August. Whoever made my tuna melt on white and Paul's malted banana-chocolate shake had a way with diner standards. Flowers spilled from planters. Nineteenth-century storefronts gleamed in the sun as if they'd been scrubbed. The few people on the street didn't look as if they'd ever roasted a possum. No one was wearing a MAGA cap. We didn't see any hounds in the back of pickup trucks. If we'd had the inclination, we could have taken a closer look at the imposing court-house with its cupola and the Neo-Romanesque heritage museum, once the home of the county sheriff. But we'd tried Casey's patience enough. Besides, we hadn't come to St. Clairsville for the architecture. We'd get our fill of that tomorrow at Fallingwater.

Road-trip days have a lulling simplicity. No laundry, no bills, no sprint to the market before dinner. How easily we'd mastered the dance. There's check-in duty (me, with Casey leaping up to collect his treat from the desk clerk) luggage-cart duty (Paul) and hotel room inspection duty (Casey, nose to carpet). The generic art could be flowers or local landmarks, the absurd strip of cloth at the foot of the bed gray or navy blue, the closest establishment an A&W or a Starbucks, but the breakfast room will always have Raisin Bran and a TV tuned to the news. Whether we're in Fox News or CNN country, each hotel returns us to some version of the same place.

At a seaside hotel on the Côte d'Azur, we once made love in a Mediterranean breeze that drifted through open French windows Matisse might have painted. In a Pittsburgh suburb, the Hampton Inn became a new kind of high point. On the road trip Casey had been the best of boys. We might have adopted one of those dogs who can't be driven to the park without howling in protest, yet Casey showed nothing but patience for our foolish human errand. He'd earned a reward. Why not let him share our bed? "The dog stays out of our bed," I had once vowed. But this was the Hampton Inn's bed. Let the pros get his paw prints off their sheets.

All night Casey slept between us. Bags clattered in the parking lot; the air conditioner hummed. With every shift of position, Casey released into the air a whiff of his distinctive pong, infusing the room with the essence of home. I put my hand on his chest to feel him breathe, my fingers brushing Paul's.

Our first day back from the trip, my phone rang in the middle of Casey's walk. "Was it beautiful?" When my friend Julian wants to talk beauty, he skips "Hi" and jumps right in. He'd caught me being dragged toward a pee-worthy tree while avoiding the turds of some other dog. Beauty was not exactly top of mind. My brain staggered momentarily.

"Fallingwater. Was it beautiful?"

"Beyond spectacular. It rises out of the woods like a castle of the forest gods. You can hear the waterfall in every room. But mortals wouldn't want to live there. No light for reading and only one chair you might be able to sit on." Julian would have relished my recap of cantilevers and mullions, but those details already escaped me.

The woman at the shelter, on the other hand, I saw perfectly—her blond bangs clipped on top of her head and her eyes on Casey's photo as she said, "I remember this dog." My last thought of our night at the Hampton Inn still warmed me. The hell with "one condition." Casey would share our bed at home; I wouldn't deprive myself any longer. Besides, I could still use a sleeping coach. We had unfinished business, Casey and I.

Pillars of the Neighborhood

I've always thought coming home from a trip is one of life's underrated pleasures. Laundry can wait. I need to get outside to walk my neighborhood again. What's in bloom outside the co-op around the corner? Have local strawberries arrived at the market? Before Casey, I looked for what was new. After, that wasn't enough. I had to see who was out on the street today—scurrying, strolling, catching the sun on a bench. My neighbors and a smattering of tourists. Odds were quite a few would see me and Casey first. People notice a fine-looking dog.

Hipster in a fedora: "I *like* you."

Streetcar driver leaning out her window: "Mwaah!"

Man with a crumpled face and rain-streaked glasses: "Nothing smells better than a wet dog."

Italian tourist: "Bravo ragazzo!"

French-speaking child, switching to English for my benefit: "You're cute!"

I'd often seen the man who rode around on a well-used bicycle, exclaiming "Fut! Fut! Fut!" He cut an incongruously dignified figure—shock of white hair like Bertrand Russell's, meditative expression. Maybe when not saying "fut" (or was it "fuck"?), he lectured at a podium and scrawled equations on a blackboard. Maybe he could quote, in Italian, 30-line chunks of *Inferno*. He struck me as a man of many gifts, not least the equanimity he projected as the only fut-futter in a community of the silent and the speaking. I watched for him—parking his bike outside my local Starbucks, inspecting Yukon Gold potatoes at the same market stall where I buy mine. If he ever noticed me, he kept it to himself. Then one morning Bike Man pedaled into view toward the end of Casey's walk, fut-futting all the way. He flashed the most exalted of smiles in our direction and called out the first intelligible, socially acceptable word I'd ever heard him say: "Hi!" He'd just given Casey and me the Halley's Comet of greetings. I should have waved at the very least, but I was too stunned to do anything except watch Bike Man disappear into the morning traffic.

There must have been a time when people laughed and pointed at him, when he longed to be like everyone else. I used to be mocked for fidgeting in class; fut-futting would have shamed me to the core. Yet on the brink of old age, Bike Man had become the best sort of local character, scattering good will by being his distinctive self.

Some of my condo neighbors had noticed him too. But they don't walk handsome dogs, so he'd never addressed them. They wondered about him, though. Bike Man wouldn't think of himself as a pillar of the neighborhood— my neighborhood for seven years—but it wasn't until he called "Hi!" that I truly felt part of things. Anyone could come this way, cruise through St. Lawrence Market and go home to Rosedale, San Francisco, London or wherever. You had to live here to know about Bike Man.

We moved to the heart of downtown from the fringes of a green and stately enclave where the bikes come from Italy and those who ride them observe the usual conventions. Former neighbors asked, "Do you miss Rosedale?" as if they couldn't understand why anyone would leave. Not so many years ago, I couldn't either. In Rosedale I watched migrating birds from my office window. Down here I look out on a low-rise jumble. The remains of a thousand and one forgotten lunches dot the sidewalk until some lucky dog cleans them up. Cranes thrust out of chasms in the ground. Fire trucks roar out of the station two blocks away. Sirens shriek; cathedral bells chime the hour. No, I didn't miss Rosedale.

I had struggled to explain myself to Rosedalians. They understand getting and spending, so that's where I tended to start. Where else could I pick up, within a five-minute walk of home, Christmas trinkets from Dollarama, sweet butter from France, a third dog bed for Casey (he needed one in every room) and that book I've placed on hold at the library (*Beloved Dog* by Maira Kalman)? My grocery store is St. Lawrence Market, rated number one in the world by *National Geographic*. Whatever I've forgotten (there's always something) could be mine before my husband noticed I had to run back over. And talk about culture: I could walk to three concert halls and more than half a dozen live theaters. Take that, Rosedale. I'd never mentioned Bike Man to any

Rosedalians, but he was one more reason to love our new neighborhood. Unlike our last, it accommodates all kinds.

From my first day here, I made space for tourists with selfie sticks, octogenarians on canes and the occasional hot shot on a skateboard. People cracked wise, sang along off-key with Spotify, summoned me to Jesus. I knew the culinary students from their clogs and checkered pants, regulars at the Deaf Culture Centre by their flying hands and animated faces. Sober professionals charged toward meetings and presentations, eyes straight ahead or on their phones. They were having less fun than anyone except the drifters engaged in a noisy argument, yet I envied them for going to an office where they could make something happen—a proposal, a presentation—and be seen to do so by their colleagues. It had been a long time since I made anything happen in the world, and without the Project I kept falling prey to a nagging sense of irrelevance.

When our local Starbucks closed, it seemed like no big deal. But Starbucks was where I used to see Bike Man park his wheels, so he stopped showing up on my corner. I thought he must be buying his coffee somewhere else, and his Yukon Gold potatoes too. It had been ages since I'd seen him at the market, or anywhere at all. While I wasn't looking, my neighborhood lost a pillar. We'd never had a conversation, yet I missed him.

Casey's new friend rode into view in an electric wheelchair. Everything about him was black—his skin, his clothes, the heavy frames of his glasses, the massive chair that barely contained his folded legs and jutting elbows. From the black bag in his lap, he pulled a Milk-Bone and held it aloft while Casey tugged wildly. The man recoiled. "Crazy puppy! He could tip me right out of this chair."

I got the feeling it had happened before. If it happened this time, I couldn't lift a man his size back into the chair. But since he wanted to present the Milk-Bone himself, we found a way. I tightened the leash and pulled; he held the treat at arm's length and leaned away from the irresistible peril that was Casey. The deep grooves in the man's cheeks made room for a smile as the Milk-Bone went down in one gulp. He introduced himself: JP, friend of dogs, proud donor of treats to the neighborhood pack. Devoted to a cat he was able to care for himself. On nearly every one of his long, tapered fingers, he wore a heavy silver ring with rune-like carvings. I meant to ask if he played the piano. "See you later," I said, hoping it would be soon. The back of the disappearing wheelchair said JP in block capitals. No one would forget the Milk-Bone man.

For years I'd been saying, "I love my neighborhood." I loved it in the offhand way I loved Montreal bagels from the market, with a faint undercurrent of superiority. If you hunted and gathered somewhere else, you weren't in the know. But then neither was I before I walked a dog and began to know my turf from within, as a neighbor among neighbors. Before, you could say hello and I'd barrel past, absorbed in thought. A man I knew slightly once told a colleague of mine, "Your boss is a real bitch." To give him his due, it looked that way.

With Casey I slowed down. He had hydrants to spray, other dogs' rear ends to inspect. He dove for bones I had to yank away from him. If he found a dead critter in the grass, which thankfully he didn't very often, he had to give it a good roll and squish. I couldn't stand apart from the world while he was pitching himself into it with paws and tail and tongue. He had to kick it up, roll in it, poke his snout into its crevices. He had to make friends who became, in the moment, my friends. The friend who made him shimmy and shake more than any other was JP.

He first entered our life on a corner between a parking lot and a playing field. No different from lots of bland urban corners, unless you've made a friend there. After that he'd turn up outside the indie coffee shop. Or we'd find him cruising along the Esplanade, where wide sidewalks made it possible, if not always easy, for someone in a wheelchair to extend a long arm in Casey's direction. JP often took a friend on his rounds, and over time he introduced us to a few. I liked to think we were pillars of the neighborhood to JP, as he was to us. When Casey jumped for the treat, JP always leaned away. Always said, with a tolerant smile, "Crazy puppy."

I had a surge of happiness at being seen by someone who was happy to see me and Casey. A few months might go by between encounters. Paul and I would take Casey south for the winter, to the turquoise bungalow with the ceiling fan on the veranda. We didn't return until the evening sky grew lighter and the snow, if we were lucky, began to recede. My first day back, I'd watch for patches of green that wouldn't last; spring comes slowly to Toronto. I'd have to wait a while for the crocuses but not for JP.

His Milk-Bones must have had plenty of takers. The area positively teemed with dogs (although I hadn't noticed until I walked my own). We had the mutt whose missing limb I didn't notice until he jumped to greet me with one front paw, the frisky slip of a thing with mismatched ears (one pointed up, the other down), the one-eyed boxer standing guard outside St. Lawrence Market. The Jack Russell terrier who barked up a storm at Casey, the submissive Samoyed who dropped down for him. Pillars of the neighborhood, to a one.

Our lone basset hound had the measured gait of an elder statesman. When I learned that he had died, and that Chester was his name, I thought of his massive paws, like the bases of Roman columns. Ave atque vale, Chester. A friend of JP's, I didn't doubt. He had to know the local dogs better than anyone, yet I never saw him treat any dog but Casey. I had no reason to think my crazy puppy came first with JP, although it seemed that way when we met on the sidewalk. If any dog alive or dead occupied that place in his heart, a multitude, including Casey, were tied for second-best.

This I knew because of my own second-best dogs, a group that comprised all my neighborhood's canine pillars. Not to be tied for second-best, a dog had to be insufferably yappy or just plain mean.

Bedmates

The last thing Casey needed was another place to sleep. He liked his dog beds fine. He liked the TV couch even better. There he could loll the night away beside his Chosen One, who preferred to sleep sitting up. A new arrangement would require a delicate touch. I should not deprive Paul of Casey's soothing presence, or Casey of his routine. He knew what he liked, and it wasn't change. He liked to walk where he had walked before, eat when he had always eaten (although earlier would please him better).

His Chosen One and I agreed that Casey would begin his night on the couch and follow me to bed a few hours later. Making this worth his while was up to me, the Other One.

Beside my pillow I placed a silk throw cushion that my late cousin Faith, an artist with her needle, had given me toward the end of her long life. An embroidered spider dances over a silvery web; pink appliquéd flowers with beaded pistils reach toward an indigo sky. Cushions attracted Casey. Faith's cushion was just the right size for his head, as if she'd made it to put him at ease.

On the first night I followed a plan. Find Casey on the couch, wake him with a gentle belly rub. Invite him to his personal cushion in the bed. We were doing fine until we got to the cushion. He was having none of it. He made a circuit of unacceptable positions: the foot of the bed (not cozy enough), behind my knees (too cozy; how was I supposed to roll over?), Paul's pillows, which became a fort within seconds but had to be kept free of drool in case the Chosen One decided to lay his head there. I shooed Casey, nudged him, pounded the silk cushion where he was meant to lie as my sleeping coach, but he knew what he wanted and the embroidered cushion wasn't it. He ran to the bedroom door and stood there, whimpering for release. Where was the unconditional love dog people carry on about?

I knew exactly how this should be. His warm chest under my hand. His breath my guide. If drool on my pillow was the price, so be it.

Breathing is the first thing anyone does in this world. You'd think it would be simple. Once upon a time, I thought so myself. Then I took a relaxation course to write a story for the first magazine that employed me. Relaxation, it turned out, was all about breathing. And I couldn't do it with ease or grace. I lay rigid on the floor—my breath strangling in my throat, my busy brain full of where to catch the bus and what to buy for dinner—as my classmates sank deeper into altered states. Sighs of release taunted me. My heart pounded like fists against a door: *Let me out of here.* I wrote the story but didn't mention my failure at relaxation. Was the failure mine or the human guru's? Casey wouldn't drone on about breathing ("Your limbs are getting heavy"). He'd let me feel the heaviness of release. All I had to do was get him into the bed.

Casey loves food, I am its keeper. I would bribe him, just once, with a treat on his embroidered cushion, like a chocolate mint in the kind of hotel we didn't frequent anymore. At first it seemed I couldn't fail. Casey heard me open the treat jar, raced after me to the bedroom, dove onto the cushion, snapped up the treat. Then bolted. Paul rolled his eyes. He didn't have to say "I can't believe what you just did." I said it to myself.

I used to laugh when dogs made chumps of their people. Once on a beach, when I thought no dog would ever be mine, I saw a galumphing Lab get the better of the woman trying to corral him. "Tigger, I'm warning you! Tigger, I'm going to count to ten! One . . . two . . . three . . ." Tigger had sand to kick up and scents to track. More than once he spun around to make sure he hadn't been forgotten. Then off he'd run while the woman wheedled, "Tigger, this is your last chance! One . . . two . . . three . . ."

Was this how she'd once talked to her misbehaving children? It had surely been a few decades since she wrangled any kids, who must have taken her orders with the same blithe disregard shown by the dog. I watched them both disappear, the leash dragging in the woman's hand as Tigger exulted in his freedom.

Poor deluded soul, she couldn't seem to grasp the difference between dogs and humans—cajoling both with a ploy that neither would buy. Now I'd caught myself making the same mistake. At bedtime Casey and I weren't Us anymore; we became a commander and a rebel. An adult human would have given me a piece of his mind; Casey gave me time to come to my senses.

When I stopped trying so hard, he stopped resisting, but his presence in the bed wasn't quite the balm I had in mind. Our bedroom looks out on a vine-covered wall that raccoons have been known to descend on their rambles. I'd seen one spread-eagled there, claws gripping the tendrils while maneuvering itself straight down with the grace of an acrobat. Casey knows raccoons as lumbering shadows never up to any good. He doesn't have to see one to know it's befouling the air. That time he woke me with a don't-try-anything bark, he might have sniffed a raccoon bound for home. I reached for his flank. *You did it, Casey. Showed that miscreant who's boss.*

Not everything he did in our bed was so welcome. The paw prints didn't surprise me, but they weren't the only sign of his presence. "Casey's left a few suspicious brown stains," I told Paul, stripping the bed that was immaculate yesterday.

"They're not at all suspicious. We know exactly what they are."

We knew and we modified our standards. No more changing the bed for a minor streak of brown on a sheet. Laundry every day? Forget it. Between clean linens and Casey, we'd take Casey. Fools for love, both of us.

"There ought to be a word for what he's reduced us to," I said. "Like 'uxorious,' only for people ridiculously nuts about their dog."

Uxorious: "excessively fond of or submissive to a wife" (thank you, Webster). Why have only wives inspired a word for excessive fondness?

"Excessive fondness for a husband is considered the default state of wives," Paul said. As for the doted-on dog, we were stumped. Maybe doting has become the default state of dog folk. Maybe lots of us put up with the odd brown stain on our sheets. Who but ourselves will ever know?

With human bedmates I'd never been a spooner. Human males have sharp knees and elbows. They don't take kindly to being pushed away. They snore a lot louder than Casey, whose faint rumble is the sound of rest. They will say, if you get up and open a window, "It's already freezing in here." After a certain age they get up and wander about in search of a more comfortable spot. Comfort blooms in Casey. All day he cultivates it, a shake and a stretch before every change of position. His downward dog flowing into the upward. When sleep falls upon him, he wants to be exactly where he is.

One night his head grazed the silk cushion and came to rest on my pillow, directly under my chin. His breath ruffled the hairs on my arm, a living breeze. I hadn't done a thing to call this moment into being, yet here we were, my hand traveling the length of his warm body. Rising and falling with his breath. In relaxation class, I compared my breath to everyone else's. They were champions, I was the laggard.

Next to Casey, I suspended judgment. I simply noticed his soft exhalation as my limbs grew heavy (so that meditation teacher had been right). My thoughts became pleasantly jumbled, like first drafts of dreams. In my last conscious thought of the night, I knew we were breathing as one.

Please Bring Him Home

The clamor of barking awoke me from a night's broken sleep with wooden bed slats digging into my back. I missed having Casey to warm my sore places like a heating pad with fur. He'd have started his day hours ago, a day like any other at the doggy farm, full of running, sniffing and chasing squirrels. My day would be the once-in-a-lifetime kind. I was going to Casa Azul, otherwise known as the Frida Kahlo Museum. The artist was born in that cobalt blue house, loved and struggled there with Diego Rivera, as brazen a philanderer as ever bewitched a woman. She died there too, after painting her way through agonies of the body and spirit. I'd seen photos of the world that awaited me at Casa Azul, Frida resplendent in embroidered gowns that celebrated Mexican tradition while concealing her wooden leg. My visit would fulfill a 30-year dream, but I felt more achy than excited.

Our below-grade Airbnb shared an alley with a dog daycare. Cheap but not cheerful was what our current budget would bear in Roma Norte, described by *Lonely*

Planet as "a bohemian enclave in the rapid process of gentrification." We'd moved in to find someone's panties hanging on an open window like a flag of defeat. The "minimalist" living room had been designed to entice trend-conscious Millennials on a website, not to cosset oldsters with complaining backs. (It contained not a single comfortable chair.) We peered through the barred front window at parading ankles and feet. Aside from location, the place had one virtue: an affable doorman. "Diego, like Diego Rivera," he said, his only stab at English. In Mexico City you needed a doorman. And bars on all your windows.

We couldn't have been closer to the subway, the grocery store, the coffee shop with vegan pastries. Yet every stroll reminded me of Casey. Tomás, a French bulldog gone missing, stared at us from scores of posters, his sagging face imperious and mournful. I knew barely enough Spanish to order breakfast, but lost-dog posters are the same everywhere. The fateful place (Acapulco and Chapultepec), the promised reward (in bold red capitals), the cry from the heart ("Please help me bring him home"). I'd never much cared for French bulldogs but I felt for Tomás and whoever was trying to recover him. So the Spanish word for bulldog is "bulldog." Unlike most of the words I was learning, this one I could remember. I might get the chance to tell someone, "What a handsome bulldog," and then tell the dog, "Good boy." That would put me almost at home.

We'd passed Tomás everywhere. Outside the seafood place we found on Yelp (the tacos looked like edible art, tasted of the ocean and gave me turista). En route to the Rivera murals that turned out to be stops and stops from the subway station we'd just exited. My fault; I'd misread the guidebook. So much for the afternoon.

Paul: "I knew I couldn't trust you to follow directions."

Me: "It was your decision to trust me."

What on earth were we doing in Mexico City? Paul didn't share my Frida Kahlo fixation, and our Someday file overflowed with places we both meant to see. As I predicted, Casey had slowed us down. Time was running out for the Hermitage, the Greek Islands, the Lake District and Vimy Ridge, where my father lost a 19-year-old brother. In a letter home, Frank Maynard had reminded young Max to take good care of Snookums, the dog.

Mexico City was the misbegotten postscript to a sojourn in San Miguel de Allende, where a generous friend had offered us the use of her villa. San Miguel had soothed us with its winding streets where bougainvillea cascaded from window ledges and the sky looked bluer than blue. Mexico City threw us into crowds, fumes and the sheer befuddlement of finding our way from here to there.

In a vast stairwell at the Palacio Nacional, we craned our necks at 500 years of Mexican history as seen by Diego Rivera: murderous conquistadores, revolutionaries hanging from gibbets, triumphant peasants raising the hammer and sickle. Rivera's vision staggered and exhausted us, like the city itself. Craving the solace of our lair in Roma Norte, we took the one chance we'd been warned not to think of taking, at the worst time we could have chosen. We boarded the subway at rush hour. While one crook shoved Paul, another reached into his pocket and made off with his iPhone.

After the theft, Paul lost heart for exploring Mexico City. Too dirty and threatening, he said. Besides, he had work to do. He set up his computer at the dining room table, there to stay until checkout, except for coffee breaks and meals. He drew the blinds. I was on my own without a dog, and I would damn well make the best of it.

My pilgrimage to Frida Kahlo's house would take more than half an hour by cab, followed by a long wait in line. Fortifying myself would require a proper breakfast. Yelp suggested the perfect spot, a neighborhood café ten minutes' walk from the apartment. Paul was snoring when I left. Diego the doorman gave me a smile and a wave. "Pablo?" he asked, miming sleep. He'd learned that Paul was not a morning person.

"Sí. Buenas días, Diego." The extent of my Spanish conversation.

At home in Toronto, I ride subway trains in the wrong direction and emerge not entirely sure which way to turn. In Roma Norte I didn't trust myself to take the fastest route to the café, even with Google Maps in the palm of my hand. If I got lost, it would be an adventure.

My route led down shady streets where colonial houses hugged the sidewalk, each one a different shade of pastel or gray. Someplace else, I might have caught a glimpse of the interiors. A chandelier, a painting, a kitchen island where someone was squeezing oranges. These houses guarded their secrets behind opaque windows—barred, as usual. I had come to a place where anything you prize can be stolen. Your phone from your pocket, your dog from wherever he was sitting one minute ago.

The day we adopted Casey, Liz warned us never to leave him tied up while taking care of some errand. He might be snatched and made to fight for his life while gamblers bet on his fate. "He's a trusting guy," she said. "He'd go with anyone." I'd often judged people harshly for leaving dogs unattended while they shopped. But anyone can think, while frazzled, "It'll be fine, just once." Hadn't Paul and I done the same when we chose to take the subway at rush hour?

Within a few blocks of my thoroughly urban starting point, where traffic whizzed at all hours and tamale stands drew lineups, I seemed to have entered a village that belonged mostly to people with dogs: little and big, sleek and shaggy, bouncing puppies and seniors with drooping bellies, all glad to be on patrol with the morning sun on their coats. Local variants of every dog I met with Casey in Toronto and had added to my second-best roster. Like Casey, they sniffed other dogs' hind ends and growled if anything seemed off. I nodded hello to passing walkers. For all they knew, I'd just dropped my own dog at home, happily spent from his rounds.

Tomás eyed me from a lamppost. I feared the worst.

Enhorabuena Café appeared precisely where Google Maps told me it would. I hadn't made one error, which gave me a frisson of pride. There was order in the world after all, accessible even to the directionally challenged. All the patrons looked like regulars taking a break from their screenplay (or was it their graphic novel?). I claimed the only table, with a prime view of the scene. "Enhorabuena" means "congratulations." (I had to look it up in my pocket dictionary.) The right word for my arrival. In halting Spanish, I ordered sweet potato hash.

Beside me sat two women old enough not to care about impressing anyone, draped and wrapped with a nonchalance that comes naturally to a seasoned few and eludes everyone else. They'd brought a honey-blond hound who was sniffing the floor for crumbs, returning to their feet for occasional neck rubs. She reminded me of Casey but longer, leaner and infinitely more polite. This dog didn't growl at kids, beg for food or put her paws on the bar. Everyone in the café knew her name: Carmela. If you called her by name, you belonged.

I didn't have to summon her. She came. While I waited for my breakfast, she rested her chin on my thigh. The sweet potato hash tasted every bit as good as it sounded, but on the pleasure scale it came second to the weight of Carmela's muzzle. I cleaned my plate; she stayed. I looked into her eyes, brown and almond-shaped like Casey's. They told me this dog was on a mission.

"She likes you," said the woman who called herself Carmela's mother. (Her English had no accent.) The second woman was the aunt.

"It's mutual. Carmela's a smart dog. She knows I miss my dog at home."

Carmela was a rescue, I learned. Dogs aren't allowed in the city's restaurants, but for a good girl like Carmela, Enhorabuena bent the rules. No, Mother wouldn't mind if I took a few photos for Facebook. (Mother. Aunt. Dog people are the same all over the Doggy Dog World.) As Carmela's chiseled face hovered over my foot, I shot a keeper.

It was time to call my Uber to Frida's house. I had one afternoon to see the paintings she kept for herself, the Mexican antiquities she collected, the table where she and Diego hosted boisterous parties, the four-poster where she painted lying down while too infirm to sit up. In Frida's lush garden, I would picture her playing with the hairless dogs and the rest of her menagerie. After her divorce from Diego, whose other women included her own sister, she painted herself in mourning—long hair cut off, a man's suit instead of a Mexican dress. The animals never let her down.

Halfway to the door, I realized I had something to tell Carmela. "What's Spanish for 'good girl'?"

"Buena chica. For a boy, buen chico."

This pleased me beyond measure. I hadn't praised a dog since we left home, and now I could.

Outside the first dog I saw was Tomás on one of his lampposts. What a homely mug, all sags and folds. But someone adored him, and that person might never get him back. I could imagine the should-haves and wish-I-hads that must be plaguing that person, every one a sign of love. I snapped a photo. Buen chico, Tomás. Buen chico.

Dog of Very Little Brain

I couldn't love Casey any more than I did, but it sometimes crossed my mind that he could be even more perfect than he was.

When Paul and I first went looking for a dog, our top priority was "smart." We thought a smart dog would be a livelier companion than a ditz, not to mention a more appropriate reflection of two humans who prized intelligence and resisted the ordinary.

Casey had one exceptional gift: He could hold his pee for somewhere around 17 hours without showing any discomfort. When home is an eighth-floor condo, pee control counts for a lot, but a mighty bladder doesn't have the charisma of a well-tuned brain. We saw no evidence of one in Casey.

I'd been checking out smart dogs on YouTube. Dogs without service training had learned to help around the house. They fetched beer, operated a snow blower, unloaded the dryer. "I wouldn't dry my hands on any towel fresh from Casey's mouth," Paul said. Well, he did want "a doggy dog," and laundry duty is not exactly doggish. The towel stunt didn't impress me either. What did was the vocabulary of a certain border collie in Spartanburg, South Carolina, who knew the names of all her stuffed toys and had a vast collection of more than 1,000. She'd proven her skills on *Nova* and in a peer-reviewed journal. Called Chaser by her family and "the world's smartest dog" by practically everyone else, she could fetch one particular stuffie from her mountain of playthings and place it as directed by her trainer and lifelong friend, John Pilley, an emeritus professor of psychology at Wofford College.

The average dog knows 165 words, nowhere close to Chaser but streaks ahead of our Casey. I could count his words without using quite all my fingers: sit, wait, walk, uh-uh, up, down, good boy (counted as one) and come (although he didn't at least half the time). We were up to eight words, nine if I threw in his name. That he knew at any volume above a whisper. He would sprint from three rooms away. "He" and "him," in the right tone of voice, had the same energizing effect. We came up with other names for the canine member of the household—Monsieur le Chien, Señor Perro, Herr Hund, Boogie Woogie Beagle Boy—but more for our own amusement than to outsmart a dog who required so little outsmarting that his name represented more than 10 percent of his entire vocabulary. Channeling Winnie the Pooh, I added one more name to the roster—Dog of Very Little Brain.

By teaching Casey one additional word, we could nudge him into double digits. We'd already identified a word that spoke to him on a primal level. He might seem absorbed in the afternoon sun on his back or the squeak of his bouncing red ball, but this word made him soar with upraised paws like a charismatic feeling the spirit. Then he'd turn tail and race to the object of his desire, the red ceramic bowl into which I was about to pour a cup of Salmon Tunalini. We hoped he was showing off his language chops, until we noticed that his rapture was pronunciation dependent. We had to roll the word on our tongues and release it with a booming flourish: "Casey, do you want DINNER?" All talk about our own dinner went right over his head. We gave the magic word our all every night, partly to share his excitement but also to prove he might be smarter than we thought.

All my life I've struggled with a bad mental habit: invidious comparisons between myself and other people who surpassed me (or appeared to) in style, achievements or brain power—the currency of Maynard Hall. I always felt better when I stopped, but the impulse died hard. Now I'd caught myself comparing our perfectly lovable dog to a canine genius and poking fun, albeit gently, when he came up short.

On YouTube I watched Chaser demonstrate her most extraordinary skill: picking out a new toy—this time a Charles Darwin doll—from an assortment of old favorites. Asked to find Darwin, she looks puzzled. She paces around her toys, then stops. You can see her thinking: *This is my game, and I'm not supposed to be flummoxed.* Told again to find Darwin, Chaser gives it her best shot. She eliminates Inky, Crawdad, Seal, Ahab, Sugar, Lover and Hamburg (imagine dreaming up names for more than a thousand toys). Into her mouth goes wild-haired, bespectacled

Darwin. Chaser's tail wags in triumph. She doesn't know she's made an inference, only that she's back on her game and all is right with the world.

I thought of Casey's last inference. Our building has a driveway that in Casey's mind belongs to the family car. All other vehicles, from cabs to delivery vans, are mere stand-ins for the only one that counts. The driveway is where I bring him down to meet Paul, who has stopped there after his errands before whisking Casey off to the dog park at Cherry Beach. Casey can't jump into the back seat fast enough. When some other car occupies the magic spot, he paws at the back door, certain Paul is at the wheel. He didn't look at all perplexed the day he scampered outside for a walk to find the driveway occupied by a tractor-size cart in a violent shade of blue. Scrapes from end to end attested to the purpose of this cart, hauling asbestos around (a crew in our building had been ripping it out). But from Casey's perspective, any vehicle in the driveway was his personal beachmobile. He tried to jump in.

It was the media, not John Pilley, who called Chaser "the world's smartest dog." In Pilley's view Chaser was not a freak of nature, putting dogs like ours to shame, but the opposite: an unwitting champion for "the genius of dogs and all species." With the right training, any dog could demonstrate remarkable talents. He wrote in his memoir, *Chaser*, "It is past time to abandon Descartes' paradigm of animals as machines and to replace it with a new paradigm of animals as truly our fellow creatures—biologically, emotionally and cognitively." Pilley had trained other dogs, but in Chaser he found one whose zest for solving problems matched his own for setting them. He was in his mid-70s when she became his Project, an endlessly compelling adventure into the mind of another species. They worked together up to five hours a day, with play as Chaser's reward because treats couldn't match the motivational power of a romp.

I had to wonder what this meant for Casey and his humans. Even if Paul and I could match Pilley's commitment to training, Casey wouldn't match Chaser's. He declined to put himself out for anything but food. Besides, Chaser was a border collie, ranked the smartest of 133 breeds in Stanley Coren's book *The Intelligence of Dogs*. Casey's dominant breed is beagle, in 126th place (ahead, in descending order, of Pekingese, bloodhound, borzoi, chow chow, bulldog, basenji and Afghan hound).

I wasn't surprised to find beagles near the bottom of the pack. Unlike Chaser and her kind, beagles are famous for a devil-may-care attitude toward commands. Coren, a psychologist at the University of British Columbia, based his ranking on a detailed questionnaire completed by enforcers of commands—the 199 judges of the American and Canadian Kennel societies. Did beagles fare badly because they're not smart or because they're not all that interested in challenges posed by humans? Any beagle worthy of the name would rather follow his nose than do almost anything else except eat.

While poking around Facebook one idle afternoon, in search of distraction from some worthy task or other, I landed on a post from the Canine Cognition Lab at the

University of Toronto. I couldn't believe my luck. The lab had just put out a call for friendly, healthy, "food-motivated" dogs to participate in studies. I knew what that meant: playing games for treats. Casey might be a Dog of Very Little Brain, but when it came to snaffling treats, I'd pit my headstrong hound against the most tractable of border collies.

I must admit to complicated motives: a little bit of high-minded interest in advancing scientific knowledge, a lot of "How smart is my dog?" Canine cognition researchers are looking at the question: What do dogs know and how do they know it? The U of T scientists belonged to a burgeoning global movement for whom the furred, scaled and feathered heads of other species have become what oceans were to Jacques Cousteau, an undiscovered world overdue for exploration. The multitude of species proving smarter than humans ever dreamed now ranges from pigs to parrots, wolves to raccoons. As research subjects, dogs offer two advantages: They're eager to please and always on offer from people like me. I couldn't wait to get Casey into a study. But between the lab's schedule and our winter trip to Florida, I waited six months for his moment.

Casey and I set out for the lab on a pleasantly brisk March morning, the kind of weather he likes best. The hospital workers on University Avenue had left a trail of sandwich wrappers waiting to be licked.

We were bound for a corner of the campus where every door opens onto a memory. The student theater where I met Paul while rehearsing *The Seagull*. (I played Masha, in mourning for her life; he was my father, the comic relief.)

The long-defunct café once famous for kaiser rolls stuffed to bursting with Mrs. Morrison's egg salad. (She seemed as old as the turrets overhead, and as timeless.) The Canine Cognition Lab sat somewhere in the dour faux-medieval building that in our day had housed the English department. (Casey's appointment was a luckier break than I knew. The lab has since moved to Brown University.)

I'd been following the rise of canine cognition as a field of serious research directed by celebrity scholars. Alexandra Horowitz of the Barnard College lab writes and illustrates best-selling books on the inner lives of dogs. Gregory Berns of Emory University, no slouch on the bestseller list himself, has trained dogs to sit in MRI scanners so he could get inside their heads. (I doubted Casey could master that skill, but maybe Berns has a special touch.) Brian Hare of Duke University has created a lucrative citizen science project called Dognition ("Find the genius in your dog"). For $79 a year, Dognition would uncover Casey's cognitive style and analyze his performance on a monthly set of "science-based" games. Paying to be part of a study, even one with the imprimatur of Brian Hare, an award-winning neuroscientist, did not sit well with me. I used to envy people who could volunteer their dogs to a university study, sometimes driving hours for the privilege. The U of T lab was a 45-minute walk from home.

You couldn't just march your dog into the lab. It was hidden away, with no receptionist to let you in. You had to be escorted to the basement room at the foot of a narrow staircase. It didn't look like much to human eyes—beige walls, video camera, a couple of folding chairs—but Casey knew at first sniff that this box of a place would be his kind of playground. He reveled in the scratches laid on by Maddie and Dolly, undergrads earning academic credit for one of their favorite things, hanging out with dogs. They seemed particularly charmed by the one now slapping their legs with his tail. "He's a Dog of Very Little Brain," I told them, hoping to be disabused of this notion.

Beside the point, Maddie explained. In these games there weren't any right or wrong answers. It mattered not at all how Casey compared to other dogs. Not to her and Dolly, anyway. The lab focused on what dogs could do as a species, not on individual differences. The study at hand explored dogs' understanding of human social cues. I didn't want to be one of those strivers who take their dog's test result personally, but returning to the campus had aroused my competitive streak.

The lab had scheduled two sessions for Casey—a warmup to get him used to its people and procedures, followed by the experiments themselves. For the warmup, Dolly placed a treat under a plastic cup in full view of Casey. All he had to do was knock the cup over. Some dogs need time to figure out the knock-and-swallow routine, but not my Casey. He aced it over and over, clever boy. When Maddie told me he was ready for the main event, two skill-testing games, I felt as if my child had skipped a grade.

Game one raised the stakes. This time Dolly placed the treat, before Casey's shining eyes, under one of two cups. Ten times out of 12, he picked the wrong cup. Worse than chance. Oh, Casey. The treat landed in his gullet anyway, and that's all that mattered to him. "If he's frustrated, we can take a break," Dolly said. Casey, frustrated? As long as Casey has a shot at a treat, count him in.

Game three started out like the last one: two cups, the treat placed under one of them while Casey watched, straining at the leash. This time Maddie took over to ensure that experience with Dolly was not affecting his response. She pointed to the cup that hid the treat, and her cue made all the difference. After failing to solve the problem on his own, Casey nailed it by reading signals from a human. "Some dogs don't seem to understand what we're asking of them when we fail to give them social cues," Maddie told me. Perhaps he'd been distracted by a busy new place, not that she could say for sure. "But I would not call Casey a Dog of Very Little Brain. He's demonstrated a fantastic ability to use human cues and I don't doubt that with skills he finds useful, he could learn very quickly."

The hour flew by. Casey would have gone on working for treats, win or lose, but Maddie and Dolly had no more games on offer.

That night the hour of expectation took its usual course. "Casey, do you want DINNER?" The entrechat, the twirl, the clatter of claws on floorboards. We would never have to say, "Isn't it time for Casey's D-I-N-N-E-R?" I knew of dogs who had learned not to fall for such tricks, but ours wasn't smart in that fashion.

He stood at his bowl, vibrating from nose to tail. Watching me reach for the tall red can that once held amaretti and now held Chicken a la Veg. He'd have to earn it. "Casey, wait." Slapdash as he was with commands, he paid close attention to this one.

Waiting asked a lot of Casey. He had to look away while his paws worked the floor and a filament of drool hung from his chin, getting longer by the millisecond. I remembered Laurie's words: "He wants to please." Indeed he did, especially when food was involved. I'd never witnessed such a naked conflict between yearning and restraint. He looked the way I feel in Pilates when all I crave is a rest but our teacher insists on more boomerangs (legs straight, "peepee muscles" tight, enough with the groaning). So what if he only knew 11 words? He had emotional intelligence. He knew I expected him to wait for his food, so he'd learned to tame his desire. When the coat and gloves came out, he knew he had a walk in the offing. But first he'd have to wait while I hunted for my phone.

Two months after our visit to the dog lab, I found a thank you from the team in my email. They'd attached three photos of Casey, shot from above, his least flattering angle. Attachment number four had me shouting to Paul, "Guess what? Casey's just received his certificate of achievement! He's a Distinguished Canine Scholar of the University of Toronto!" I'm not sure what became of the U of T diplomas awarded to the humans in our family, but Casey's certificate appeared on Facebook for all to see. No mention of his course of study, as if we had to ask. Casey was the world's ranking expert on us.

Appetite

Paul had a bone to pick with me. More precisely, a chunk of two-day-old hamburger he'd found in the compost bin. How could I have thrown it away?

My husband likes to snack. If our fridge contains the crispy end of a broiled flank steak, or a scoop of pasta with garlic and bacon, he'll make sure it's not forgotten. If there's nothing on offer but shriveled lemon wedges and bits of shallot wrapped in plastic, he stands there looking bereft. "I can't understand why you save some of the stuff you do," he said, "and not a third of a perfectly decent burger."

That burger had once been more than decent, laced with grated cheddar and salsa. Once, but not anymore. "It was no prize. Who'd eat a nubbin of cold burger?"

Paul gave me his you've-forgotten-something look. This time what I'd forgotten wasn't a receipt I should have saved or a phone message from his optometrist. "What about Casey? It suited him fine. He'd have liked it even better with two days' aging."

I've always believed the right amount to eat is somewhat less than you'd like. I am leery of snacks, third helpings and covert efforts to even up the corners of the leftover potato leek gratin meant to grace another meal. If Melissa Clark says her gratin serves six, I figure it should make four servings for me and my trencherman husband, beside a smoked beef sausage or two. Any cook who'd drench her gratin in a full cup of cream and nearly as much Gruyère can't be all that abstemious, but my husband still says as I tuck half of it in the fridge (really just shy of half, so the leftovers won't disappoint), "Nothing wrong with that another helping wouldn't fix." Portion control has been a sore point between us. With Casey's arrival I found myself outnumbered.

Casey always wanted more—from the sidewalk, from the treat jar, from our dinner plates, from any patch of ground where crumbs had been left for the birds. I had learned to ask friendly strangers, their hands extended to pet him, "Are you carrying food? He might try to steal it." He would hover near the table as we ate, waiting for Paul to dangle a chunk of salmon skin. It disappeared in one gulp.

"Snacking at the table isn't good for dogs. You're encouraging an unhealthy habit." I invoked higher authorities. Our vet, books and articles by vets. Did Paul know that more than half of dogs are obese—candidates for heart disease, diabetes and arthritis? Did he want our dog to die before his time or suffer needless pain in his dotage?

"Well, I asked Casey about that salmon skin, and he thinks I made the right call. If you had your way, he'd be the world's first canine anorexic." Casey thumped his tail against the chair leg and nudged Paul's thigh with his nose. Nothing wrong with that piece of salmon skin that more wouldn't fix.

Casey learned fast who made the right calls around here—by his lights, anyway. He figured out that I eat the whole banana myself, while Paul saves a chunk for his sidekick. If Casey happens to be walking with me or cavorting with his kind at daycare, the chunk still goes into his dish. A principled man, my husband. Also an adept peeler of bananas. I didn't know how softly a banana could be peeled until I watched Paul do it at the kitchen counter. He had honed this move for a sharp-eared audience of one who at that moment was nowhere to be seen. Casey ran from the bedroom to drool at Paul's feet for his prize—the banana end he would catch in the air, his only trick. "And you wonder why I'm his favorite," Paul said.

I had another way to show my love. Before bed I brushed his teeth, on orders from Dr. Bob. It's not fun but someone has to do it or he might have a toothless old age. Casey tolerates my fingers at the back of his mouth, where Dr. Bob prescribes extra vigilance. He's sweet enough not to bite me, which I take as a sign of trust. But when it comes to signs of love, he'll take banana chunks—or better yet, salmon skin—over toothpaste tricked out as peanut butter and thrust against his molars with a hard piece of plastic.

In his first days with us, Paul felt that Casey wasn't getting enough to eat. Why else would a dog devour so much garbage? He put the question to a dog-loving friend. Said this man of Casey's appetite, which he considered perfectly normal, "His idea of eating enough is until he throws up."

As the keeper of the kibble, I measured Casey's portion with a plastic cup from Dr. Bob, who kept a close eye on his weight. Paul was the keeper of the good stuff: chicken gristle, sour cream spoons, the last licks of cream cheese in the container, which Casey would scour with his tongue until it looked fresh from the dishwasher.

Two of a kind, Casey and Paul. Casey skims the kitchen floor with his nose, hoping for stray bits of cheese (if only he'd mop up the potato peel while he's at it). Paul stands in front of the open fridge, looking for a toothsome morsel I hadn't bought lest I invite temptation.

I sometimes thought our ever-hungry dog was my husband's alter ego. After one of their outings in the car, Paul would tell me Casey's choice of lunch spot. "Casey said, 'Let's go for fish and chips and I can help you eat the fries.'" "Casey said, 'Let's stop at the ice cream parlor so you can have a milkshake and get me a kiddie cup.'"

Fries. Kiddie cups. Not on my watch.

An old man called to us from a bench at Corktown Common. He held out a plump sandwich wrap that set Casey twirling. "Pita. Good stuff. For your dog."

"Please, just a bite," I said. "I'm watching his weight."

The old man chortled (he did a lot of that). This line about weight would get me nowhere. Casey had wedged himself between the man's thighs and was rubbing his upturned head against his would-be benefactor's belly. Down went the palm-size chunk of pita.

Some things are so important, they must be repeated with invisible exclamation marks. For this man it was "Pita! Good stuff" in an Eastern European accent. He threw the whole thing on the ground, untouched, except for the corner he'd just shared with Casey, who could barely contain his excitement. Egg salad overflowed the pita. I tightened my grip on the leash. "Sir, that's terribly generous of you, but I can't let him eat that."

The more I talked, the more he laughed. He didn't seem to know much English but he got my drift and it amused him. He and Casey were in cahoots. They both knew how this would end.

The pita lay on the ground, sending whiffs of egginess to Casey's twitching nose. The old man had just given up most of his breakfast. It seemed wrong to refuse his offering. What was the harm?

Casey looked up, wagging, from the spot where the pita had been. No more? The stranger held up his empty hands. When he smiled, you'd think he had received the gift.

The Casey Effect

I'd never met so many men as I did with Casey. For some dog walkers, that's the whole idea. Dog parks show up on most lists of where to meet single men, and I didn't even have to make it all the way to the park. We walked, men approached, although few looked like date material. They were men with lank hair under soiled baseball caps. Men with shopping carts that held their worldly goods. Men who hung around smoking outside the methadone clinic, or waited for the streetcar on one of downtown's rougher corners, where the storefronts have rusty iron grills and only the pigeons look well fed. They do a lot of waiting, these men. They wait for a square meal and a place to bed down for the night. They wait for a friend to pass by. When a sprightly dog approaches with cuddle-me eyes, they can't wait to get their hands on him. I told Paul, "If anything happens to you, I'll have plenty of takers, thanks to Casey. And they'll all be down and out."

I've known women who attract male attention while pushing a grocery cart or laughing with a friend on the streetcar. They might not be the greatest beauties in sight, but they look like they could put a guy at ease over a beer. I look like I'd correct his grammar and ask if he needs that side of fries. Except when Casey is beside me.

Paul had also noticed the Casey effect, but with him it took the opposite form. He'd never met so many pretty young women going places or doing their best to look the part. I knew the type: fresh pedicure, Kate Spade handbag, big smile for any pert dog who happens by. At lunch hour they sit in pairs on park benches, takeout grain bowls balanced on their laps. When Casey tries to steal their lunch, they coo and cluck. Paul had a surefire quip for such moments: "Always the dog, never the owner!" He might be a portly sexagenarian but he knew more than most whippersnappers about putting women at ease. For him the Casey effect meant a moment's flirtation that amused because it was complete in itself. No coffee date, no exchange of contact details, no hand brushing hand, just two people enjoying each other on the fly.

I envied him that. My version of the Casey effect came with a melancholic shiver. Around any corner, I might meet a man consumed by hunger—for the touch of a living creature, for a chance to be the One for a love long gone or never found. It was a new way of moving through the world, one that pulled me into lives I could neither change nor forget. In the eyes of these men, I had it all: glasses that weren't taped together, clothes that didn't come from a charity, the more-or-less rested look that follows at least a few hours' sleep in a bed of my own. And I had a blithe dog at my heels. If they thought I seemed full of myself, it wouldn't surprise me. They never asked me for anything except a little time with Casey. Yet these chance meetings felt personal. They led somewhere I hadn't expected to go.

Five minutes or so from home there's a convenience store where men gather, leaning against its rusty grill. Ads for lottery tickets and legal services cover the store window like a dusty curtain. The Queen streetcar stops at the door but the men aren't waiting for a ride. We happened to pass by one day after Casey's checkup at the vet's, and he was feeling particularly chipper after coaxing extra treats from the receptionist. A call rang out from behind us: "Hey! Come and say hello!"

I took a good look at our would-be friend. Probably at most 35 but leaning on a cane. Skinny, with a gut that overflowed the waist of the gym shorts that he wore to hold up a baggy pair of long johns. He held out his arms and Casey jumped into them. I had tried to enforce a strict no-jumping rule, but in our part of town muddy paws and a sloppy tongue might be the highlight of someone's day. People craving Casey's jump should get it, I decided. For everyone else, I'd yank him back. "Be consistent," Laurie had said; I was anything but. That day Casey jumped with the zest he usually reserves for anyone carrying food. This man had none. "He likes to have his butt scratched," I said.

"Me too. Been a while, though." When he grinned, I saw the spaces where teeth used to be. He could handle a dog's rear end like nobody's business. Casey twirled and thumped against his thigh, beseeching him not to stop.

"What's his name, sweetheart?" I'd delivered some stern lectures to men who call me "sweetheart" or the equally odious "dear," but this was not a teachable moment. When I told him Casey's name, he lit up. "Casey Jones! Like that Grateful Dead song!" As the Dead sang it, Casey was high on cocaine and should've watched his speed. The man began to sing off-key about trouble everywhere. Around us men shot the breeze, smoked, high-fived passing buddies. One had brought a stool to perch on and make a day of it. The Dead fan seemed to occupy a different world, swaying to the music in his head. Of all the men who might have stopped us that day—Cobain fans, rap fans, guys who weren't into music—I happened to have met a Grateful Dead fan who'd treasure this detail. My grandmother had a Yiddish word for such moments: "beshert," fate.

The Dead fan pulled Casey closer, as if he felt beshertness in his bones. The two of them were nose to nose, eye to eye, Casey wagging up a storm. "Casey Jones!" he said. "How about that? Casey, do you love me?"

The Dead fan called himself our neighbor. But I didn't want to be neighborly with him or any of the drifters who befriended Casey. They unnerved me with their fragility, their hunger for acceptance. I never thought, of some lost soul hailing Casey, "How like my father." Not consciously, at least. My father dressed like an English gentleman. Seersucker blazer, daffodil-yellow tie, cashmere socks that he wore even as the heels gave out (my mother kept an eye on expenses). You wouldn't guess that in his cups, he phoned colleagues and friends to berate them for failures of moral courage or imagination, thereby dodging the memory of his own failures.

He didn't speak of his missteps, yet at three or four I could sense them. My father liked to sing to me then. The song I still hear, in his mournful baritone, is "The Streets of Laredo." I used to ache for the "poor cowboy" who's wasted his life gallivanting in the saddle and knows he's done wrong. Now he lies dying, "cold as the clay." I was too young to recognize my father in the cowboy.

When I started walking Casey, my father had been dead for more than 35 years. Poor cowboys, though, kept reappearing. The one who trained him at the prison in St. Clairsville. The ones who hailed us on the streets of Toronto. The one I refused to see but couldn't banish altogether, hard as I tried, because of his claim on my family and his boundless affection for Casey—Paul's dissolute cousin Adrian.

Best Friends

When Casey met Adrian, he recognized his kind of guy. If a couple of JP's Milk-Bones could win Casey's heart, imagine the impact of two giant, meal-size hamburger patties, Adrian's idea of a nosh between meals. I didn't witness this gift or the exultation that followed; I'd already built a wall between me and Adrian. No visits, no calls to our home phone number. He was too sweet-natured not to like, but I didn't want trouble. Adrian was trouble. Everything about him was big—his frame, his voice, his appetites, his bottomless need. He had lost a child, failed at relationships, trusted the wrong people. Someone always had to save him from crisis. He turned to Paul, the only person in his life not working an angle.

Until drugs and alcohol wiped him out, he carried thousands of dollars in his wallet and sent me extravagant presents in the hope of winning me over (a set of nonstick cookware I didn't need, a too-heady scent I never wore, in a bottle shaped like Barbie's torso). He doted on a houseful of cats, his greatest love in the world. After losing his cats along with everything else, he bounced between shelters and woebegone bachelor apartments. The sound of his voice on Paul's cell phone—I could hear it from across the room—always made my stomach tighten. What did he need this time? If not a few hundred dollars, then a ride somewhere. Home from jail, home from detox, home from the hospital after a close call with flesh-eating disease. When the landlord kicked him out, he needed moving assistance. It seemed he could bounce back from anything to flirt with women (despite the loss of a chunk of his arm, he looked surprisingly hale) and chide Paul about his weight. Adrian lived more than an hour's drive from our place. After taking care of the day's emergency, Paul would treat him to fish and chips, maybe a burger and a beer. A twenty to help tide him over until the pension check arrived. Adrian was like a floundering child of 60-something who could keep on courting trouble for some years yet.

"A beer?" I always said. "He's an addict. You're feeding his illness."

"You're such a hard-ass." Damn right I was, and I had a good reason. With my father, I'd already given up enough to addiction. Paul didn't always say yes to Adrian's pleas for money, but the handouts added up, and we argued about them. Money for drugs and booze, as far as I was concerned. I could no sooner feel charitable toward Adrian, who showed no interest in sobering up, than he could become a Buddhist monk. I couldn't tell which I resented more, the financial cost of this bond or its emotional pressure on our household. Adrian looked forward to visits with Paul, but Paul often came home feeling drained by the insistence of Adrian's need and the hopelessness of his situation. Knowing Adrian's love for animals, he sensed that Casey would lighten things up.

On the day of the patties I took the evening walk. Ten minutes along, Casey's bowels exploded a few steps from someone's front door. No scooping that mess into a bag, or even an entire roll of bags. It spread across the pavement, a rank puddle of shame. I cursed Adrian for making Casey sick, and Paul for not stopping the pig-out. How unjust that I was now the one on cleanup duty in the dark.

I meant to beg forgiveness and a roll of paper towels from the person whose walk had been defiled, although the prospect made me cringe. For all I knew that person hated dogs for precisely this kind of behavior. When nobody answered the door, I saw my chance to clean up the mess before anyone was the wiser. How hard could this be?

I dragged Casey to the one variety store within striking distance. Barged past the pictogram of a dog with a red slash through it, declaimed my tale of guilt to the recoiling store owner and his gaggle of customers. "Paper towels! Please, I need paper towels before someone steps in the poop puddle my dog just left outside their house!" The owner couldn't wait to be rid of me. He thrust a roll of towels into the crook of my elbow, but there's nothing quick about a one-handed purchase when you're rooting through your wallet, and at the same time yanking on the leash because your scamp of a dog has just found the salted peanuts.

While handing over all the cash I had, I longed to tell the assembled witnesses that the goofball in their midst was not the real me. The real me had her act together. The real me, not so long ago, presented in boardrooms, bright and shiny as the brass buttons on my red bouclé suit (which, to be honest, I hadn't squeezed into since the glory days of the Concorde). People used to listen as the real me held forth on the strategic plan for *Chatelaine*, but Casey wouldn't listen to the word "no."

This was the real me now, a clueless intruder in a drool-stained jacket, beating a retreat from the peanut rack while silently praying to whatever gods there be, "Please, let no one in this store ever see me again."

At least no one saw me on my knees, attacking the stain with disintegrating wads of paper towel. No one except Casey, who deemed me unworthy of notice. He'd picked up a scent emanating from a thicket where some rodent lurked. He pushed his snout deep into the branches, tugging the leash just shy of its breaking point. At last I staggered to my feet, numb from crouching, with nothing to show for my pains but a bagful of stinking paper towels. *Oh, Casey. You've made me absurd.*

I gave Paul a piece of my mind. "Tell Adrian he doesn't have to buy Casey's love. Casey knows who loves him." That he did. Forever after, the sight of Adrian made Casey break into a jig. I never saw the excitement; that would have meant seeing Adrian. But Paul would describe the scene.

Casey likes big men with big voices and big, energetic hands all over him. Especially when they share their fries. It had been years since Adrian could go shopping for a gift with the power to thrill someone. He offered Paul what his budget would bear, head-scratching oddities of unknown provenance (coupons on the point of expiry, candy bars past their best-before date). Casey he could thrill. Food did the trick every time.

I thought of Adrian when I passed the scene of Casey's accident. The stain persisted for weeks, a brown reproach. I'm not sure when it finally disappeared or even where it used to be. I found myself missing that blotch I couldn't scrub away. It put me in mind of graffiti scrawled under a bridge by intoxicated teens who think they've invented love. Except Casey and I didn't put it there ourselves, not really. The instigator was Adrian.

Every time he called Paul, he asked after "CJ," his own personal nickname for Casey. As a Jones, he liked the reminder that he and our dog were family. I still wanted nothing to do with the poorest cowboy of them all, yet his devotion to Casey had begun to weaken my defenses. He made so many calls that Paul missed a few or chose not to pick up. I remember a voicemail that boomed with the heat of inspiration. Casey's name had been on Adrian's mind. Our dog should have a middle name, Charles (their grandfather's name and Paul's middle name). Casey Charles Jones. Since when does a dog need a middle name? I had to admit it, though. Casey Charles Jones had a ring to it.

No one knows for sure when Adrian overdosed. If not that day, then not long after. My first reaction was relief, my next a startling burst of gratitude. While I hadn't wanted Adrian in my life, I could be glad he'd been part of Casey's, making my dog happy and receiving in return what might have been the happiest moment of his own day. Casey Charles Jones never looked for Adrian. He is, after all, a dog. Out of sight, out of mind, except with the most profound attachments. But if Adrian could spend one more afternoon with Casey, bearing fries or not, he'd be welcomed like the truest friend a dog ever had.

My softening to Adrian reminded me of a flower I'd never noticed or heard of until Casey peed on one. Shape of a morning glory, size of a violet, some white, others the palest pink. I took a photo for my Facebook page. Could anyone tell me what it was? There are apps for this, but I trust the knowing eyes of botanically minded friends.

I had found my first bindweed, a tough little plant known for long and powerful roots. Cursed by gardeners for choking flowers and shrubs, bindweed can thrive anywhere, even downtown sidewalks. Concrete only looks impenetrably hard; it's full of microscopic cracks. In go the roots of the bindweed, on they push until the sidewalk buckles. Up comes the flower I nearly trampled once. On Casey's walk I took photos of peonies and roses that had been watered, staked, fertilized, but I didn't keep them. Those photos told no stories. The bindweed shots I kept, a virtual bouquet for Adrian.

Catch Me While You Can

The only camera I possessed was the one in my aging phone. It nestled in my dog-walking kit between the treats and the poop bags, light enough to forget until Casey stopped for a pee. While he let loose (and kicked up dirt to spread his scent around), I would take a good look at wherever we found ourselves. It could be a place we'd been many times, as recently as yesterday, but it never looked quite the same twice. Jews ask at the Passover table, "How is this night different from all other nights?" I began to ask, "How is this walk different from all other walks?" My neighborhood had a pulse and moods. Almost every day something new caught my eye. It seemed to whisper, "Over here. Catch me while you can."

Three red apples positioned in a water fountain—an impromptu still life.

A neighbor's riff on a rock garden: painted stones depicting flowers, mushrooms, musical notes, mini-abstractions and the warning "All my rocks are cursed. Do not take."

The wind perusing a paperback copy of *The Black Rood: Book 2 of the Celtic Chronicles* left on a trash bin, minus its cover (my first video).

The last sage of summer, which I hadn't noticed till the end of November. Still green although the forecast called for snow.

In the window of a row house with a battered front door, a sign that proclaimed what a very, very, very fine house it was.

New leaves transformed into white blossoms by April snow about to melt.

A bouquet of white peonies, slashed with red at the hearts, tossed aside on the Queen Street Bridge.

Around my own neighborhood with Casey, I took more photos than I had anywhere on our travels. No shot of mine could evoke the Grand Canyon or the soaring stained-glass windows of la Sainte-Chapelle, but my phone and I did well enough with the whimsical, the modest, the abandoned. My discoveries held no appeal for Casey, yet I owed them all to him.

Before we found Casey, a friend advised me that female dogs make better walkers. Males dillydally. They keep stopping to pee and mark. You want to make time, you don't choose a male. This friend had raised many dogs and knew her stuff. I thought of her when I heard a woman say, to a dog letting fly against a tree, "You've got *more* in there? Seriously?" I came to appreciate the shillyshallying. Casey was giving me photo ops, although I had to click fast. If I didn't, he'd pee on a tulip bed or lick something even more foul than garbage.

My photos had no artistry. Some I deleted; the best I cropped and posted on Facebook, a journal of my travels with Casey. It gave me solemn pleasure to preserve the memory of our wanderings, each one a stand-in for anyone's walk, in any ever-changing neighborhood. I found myself introduced at gatherings as "Rona, who writes the most amazing Facebook posts." So this is what I'd become. A Facebookist. (Facebooker?) All very well, but not the Project.

A Matter of Burning Importance

When you dress for a dog, it doesn't matter what you wear. Too-cool-for-drool capri pants hung untouched, all shoes without rubber soles had been kicked to the back of the closet. My sensible nylon purse held a nub of a lipstick once in a while, and a roll of poop bags without fail. But to dine with sister members at the signature conference of a Very Important Association, I dusted off a tangerine silk jacket and found some mascara not yet dried out. This group didn't take fashion lightly. There would be Prada, Manolos and serious jewelry. For the first time in recent memory, I had treat crumbs nowhere on my person.

The Very Important Association was the last remnant of my former life. They do not recruit women whose most consequential meeting of the day is with their dog. They seek the connected and esteemed, but let the Formerly Important stay on. When I was invited to join, at the peak of my magazine career, my initial flush of pride gave way to mild annoyance that I'd been overlooked to that point.

Was I considered less important than a managing partner in a law firm or an EVP at a bank?

Such illusions I had.

At a candlelit table overlooking the Boston skyline, dressed as someone I used to be, I took my place among a coterie of women at the peak of their change-making powers. None of us had met before and we had little time to get acquainted, but this group excelled at cutting to the chase. One by one, each woman recounted her milestone of the year: a vision realized against the odds, a lifelong passion repurposed as a lucrative career.

They dazzled me, these women. How bold they were, how tenacious. In their spare time they sat on boards, advised candidates for office, launched charities to do what had never been done. They groomed protégées to soar at least as high as themselves. Did they ever sleep?

Even when I ran a magazine, I often felt outclassed by the titans of the VIA. Now I didn't run a thing. Each of these women had a place beyond home where she belonged, where people struck sparks with her and looked to her for answers. The table talk had me longing for a place I too could go to make things happen, although the office that used to be mine wasn't anywhere I wanted to be. They'd been slashing the budget and laying people off.

The Boston skyline twinkled. A server bent to refill my glass. What milestone could I share? Instead of launching the Project, I'd been ambling around with Casey in jeans and scuffed hiking boots. Kibitzing with JP, taking photos of bindweed. Our daily outing produced a bag of poop and two happy walkers. My turn had come to speak. "My husband and I got a dog. He's transformed our lives."

The women whipped out their phones. Heads bent, fingers flew. *A dog! Where would we be without our dogs?* Round the table went the phones, each one displaying a photo of someone's adored pup. I fumbled for a shot of Casey—any shot would do—while exclaiming at the Yorkie in a Christmas sweater and the Lab snuggling with a grandchild, but I was too slow off the mark. As a straggler phone made its rounds, the woman beside me muttered, "Corgis! Nasty little dogs." With both hands free at last, I found a shot of Casey surveying Corktown common—paws on a bench, nose uplifted for a scent. I'd caught him in a rare moment of almost-nobility. But the conversation had moved on. I slipped the phone back into my purse, Casey unremarked.

When news broke that I was leaving *Chatelaine*, my friend Audrey called to let me know I'd regret it. No pleasantries; she came straight to the point. "So how does it feel to be finished with the most important thing you'll ever do?"

My grip tightened on the receiver. "Who says I'm through with important things? I'm not even 55 yet. I've got years ahead. It's time to surprise myself."

I might as well have told her I'd enrolled in clown school. "Look, have you realized how tough this transition will be? You're used to being a Very Important Person. The day you walk out of your office is the day a lot of people stop returning your call. And I don't think you're going to like being Formerly Important."

Typical Audrey, ever the blunt-spoken lawyer. Clients pay her handsomely to keep them out of trouble; I was getting the full Audrey treatment for free. "About time I found out who my real friends are."

In the vanished days of my Importance, many people acted like friends. My job preceded me into cocktail receptions, exuding the aura that eclipsed the private me. Strangers thought they already knew me from my airbrushed photo at the front of *Chatelaine*, my smile at the elusive midpoint between welcoming and folksy. "I love your column!" they'd say, clasping my hand. Somebody once murmured, on her way to the bar, "You are a national treasure!" I could never be sure whether all these new friends were speaking from the heart or about to ask me for a favor—a *Chatelaine* table at their gala, a story on their client, a summer job for their daughter, who was acing English at McGill.

Until *Chatelaine* wrapped me in its luster, Importance was not in my sights. I had been the child who spent recess by herself, the 16-year-old never kissed except by the gay friend trying to be straight. Becoming the center of attention seemed such an odd deviation from my natural state that I was certain it would never turn my head. Then constant reminders of Importance chipped away at my resolve. New ones landed on my desk every day in the form of gilt-edged invitations to swanky parties. The most memorable of these—on the heaviest vellum, with multiple layers of envelope—had to be disassembled, not simply opened. The Queen was coming to Toronto. I'd been summoned to dine with Her Majesty at the Royal York.

The Queen had never interested me, but by this time Importance did. I thought I'd received a rare honor—until I realized every second person in my circle had received the same invitation. An acquaintance of mine received a call from an ever-so-formal gentleman who introduced himself as the royal protocol officer, with instructions on how she should dress. The woman grabbed a pen: blue shoes, square black purse, triple strand of pearls. And the finishing touch: a pin in the shape of a Corgi. She suddenly remembered it was April 1. A prankster friend was having her on.

I don't mean to make fun of this woman. The truth is, I'd been having style conniptions myself. (Was the black jersey too somber? The purple velvet too ostentatious?) "I can't believe you're in a tizzy over this," said Paul, who was also on the guest list but recognized a corporate duty call. I envied his composure. The perception of Importance had unraveled me.

Flying home from Boston, I slipped into a reverie. I saw myself at the enormous desk of my Very Important years. Behind me, the Toronto skyline at dusk, every pinprick of light an office where people strove to make partner, make the numbers, make "the next level." Before me, perched on a narrow-backed chair, a young editor named Emily. She had drive, talent, everything it would take to land a job like mine one day. Without any warning, she'd given notice.

She was following her fiancé to Northern Ontario, where he'd found work as a wildlife biologist. Okay, so she loved him. That I understood. The sticking point was Northern Ontario. Didn't we have plenty of wildlife in downtown Toronto, ripping into the garbage every night with eager paws? What would Emily do in Nowheresville? What if the marriage broke up, leaving her with no job or recent work experience? Surely I could talk her out of this.

The plane banked above Toronto. Below me I could make out the campus where I had met Paul and the downtown streets I used to glide through in a cab, on my way to nibble smoked salmon canapés with people who seemed important at the time. I'd forgotten most of that crowd but could still picture Emily, looking like a child hauled into the principal's office—head lowered, hands twisting in her lap as I launched into my notion of a heart-to-heart: *You can go anywhere you want in this business, but the next few years will be critical. You'll have lots of opportunities here. Don't throw your future away.*

Rewinding the scene, I couldn't make out one word from Emily. How could it be otherwise? I hadn't been listening. When tears welled up in Emily's eyes, I thought she'd come to her senses. More likely she wept because much as she'd relished her job, she felt the tug of another way of life. And I hadn't acknowledged her pain. Perhaps even worse, I'd sent the clear message that the life she was choosing didn't matter half as much as the one she could have by following my example. There's a look I get when I don't like what I'm hearing. Raised eyebrow, frozen lips. I'm told it's a chiller.

Emily went off to Northern Ontario and set up shop as a freelance writer. She didn't want a career like mine; she wanted time for hiking and canoeing. She wanted open spaces for her kids to explore. And as it turned out, she wasn't ditching any opportunities. By the time I fell out of love with my job, the public was falling out of love with magazines. Everything I'd built at work was about to become something else or vanish entirely. The mission statements and strategic plans went into a big yellow dumpster. I tossed them in myself, like handfuls of earth into the grave of who I used to be. I had relished most of my time in that office, but how important was it in the grand scheme of things? Why should casting a line into a river with your child matter less than presenting at the sales conference?

Showing Up

My Facebook post on Casey's last walk had taken some time to come together, and I still had things to do before his next one. Order that purse I'd had my eye on, check the online reviews of a TV series on our might-watch list. Google poems by a poet I'd never heard of until the *New York Times* informed me she had died. Casey was waiting on our best-traveled strip of carpet. Next time I made a move, I'd have to walk around him. There he lay, the picture of canine forbearance—head between paws, one haunch raised and ready for action. His window-facing ear slid back to catch rumblings of alarm or promise that only a dog can hear. But it was the eyes that got me, tracking my morning circuit between couch, kitchen and laundry room. Amber pools of longing under brows that lifted and fell with his hopes. If dogs could count, he'd be counting all my wasted steps at home, when outdoors the wide world was calling.

We were in for the worst kind of summer weather, heat radiating off the sidewalks. Not the lowest level of dog-walking hell—that would be ice pellets in our faces, followed by puddles of rain in my shoes—but close enough. I should have leashed Casey up first thing, before the air turned clammy.

Sometimes in the corridor we'd cross paths with our neighbor, Pete, and his sheepdog mix, Bandit. Pete always shook his head at Casey's walking regimen. "We're just going around the block," he would say. In the best of circumstances, Pete found Bandit's walk more burden than pleasure, but at least he showed up for his dog.

Many don't, perhaps the majority. As the studies tell it, somewhere between 40 and 60 percent of dog folk are slackers. Maybe they turn the dog loose in the yard, maybe they hire a walker. Either way, they're missing something. The late Sam Simon, animal-rights activist and co-creator of *The Simpsons*, once said with Simpsonian brashness, "I don't get why anyone would want a dog walker. It's like paying someone to fuck your wife." Simon lived in Pacific Palisades, California. No ice pellets there. But still.

Pete seemed to think I was a dog-walking martyr. From time to time I thought so myself. But the truth is, I needed to show up for someone. Paul didn't count. He could go where he chose when the spirit moved him. We were around for each other, but aroundness has no shape or boundaries and gives no rhythm to the day. Only showing up can do that.

While I ran a magazine, I showed up every day for my staff. Without me, nothing happened of note. The vacancy was not filled, the cover not approved, the plan not confirmed for the next year's issues. Others could have answered the emails from readers, but I set great store by the personal touch, especially with the affronted and aggrieved, whom I came to know collectively as Mrs. Outrage. Mrs. Outrage had many real-world names and addresses but she always signed herself "Mrs." She went to church and had a horror of sin, but when she canceled her subscription she let the profanity fly. When I wrote to Mrs. Outrage, I imagined we were sitting face-to-face. I made no promises I didn't intend to keep, but let her know a real person had heard her and felt for her, this woman adrift in a world she no longer recognized, where gay people could marry and women flaunted their cleavage at Walmart. Often she'd write back to say, "I'm sorry I shot my mouth off. I didn't think anyone would read my letter. I still don't agree but thanks for writing." What she wanted most from me was the simple courtesy of showing up.

Long after I left that job, people asked me what I missed, thinking it had to be the trappings of glamor—orchestra seats to the show of the season, invitations to Important parties. They never saw me eating cold pizza while composing a letter to Mrs. Outrage. What I missed was what everyone misses who once loved a job and left, whether they taught kindergarten or worked on a shop floor. I missed showing up for the funny and the grave, the cranky and the preternaturally cheerful, my team at the office and the readers far and wide. They all needed me until I closed my office door for the last time. Then they needed someone else instead.

Casey had become my team of one, or was it the other way around? He had a mission and unless I took him out, he would fail. He had to make sure that the rodents weren't getting out of line and no half-eaten burritos went to waste. This, not mere elimination, was the true nature of his business. If Casey could speak, he wouldn't call this ritual of ours a walk. From his perspective we were on patrol.

While trotting, he scanned the ground with the concentration of a seasoned worker absorbed in that state of being known to humans as flow. He got to fulfill his purpose, I got to witness his zest. He never made a kill, although I saw him come close among the crumb-fattened pigeons of Queen Street East. He charged, then leaped with open jaws as they rose in a clamor of wingbeats and a cloud of feathers. From his lower lip I pulled his trophy: a single white feather, tipped with gray. He looked back but not for long. It was as if he'd never terrorized those pigeons.

My walks with Casey had a kind of background music, not sung but chanted to a beat that felt as natural as breath. Over and over I'd repeat the same two words: "Good boy." I spoke them so softly that no one we passed would realize I was speaking. At first I didn't realize it myself. Maybe Casey heard me, maybe not. There was always so much else to hear. Shrieks of children, rumble of the streetcar, thump of a basketball on the rim of a net. If we timed it right on a Sunday morning, hymns drifting from Little Trinity Church. As we left our busy neighborhood behind, the sounds of human life give way to bees and birdsong. I said, "Good boy," not so much to Casey as to myself, the trees and the sky.

"Good boy you got there," some passerby might observe.

"Except when he isn't." Code for "He makes his share of mischief, and I love him for it."

As interspecies conversation goes, mine with Casey was decidedly minimal. I have friends who never leave home without asking a pet to hold the fort. One woman sings original songs to her cats. Several enact two-way conversations (they unburden themselves, the pet "replies" in a special voice). I didn't even bother much with commands beyond "sit" and "wait." I liked saying "Good boy," so I kept saying it, unless Casey lunged at a toddler. It had a reassuring Biblical solidity. The Book of Genesis: ". . . and God saw that it was good." Psalm 23: "Surely goodness and mercy shall follow me all the days of my life." The more I spoke of Casey's goodness, the more inclined I felt to do a little good.

You can't walk a dog in the city without meeting lonely people. The Beatles wondered, in "Eleanor Rigby," where they all come from. The young man with the intense dark eyes and the nose ring must have traveled far to St. James Park. He asked, in a mysterious European accent, "What kind of dog is that?"

"He's a mutt. Little bit of lots of things, more beagle than anything else."

He pondered this for a bit, as if searching his brain for the file to contain my dog. "Beagle" wouldn't do for this man. He had to make the connection between the unknown dog at his feet and everything he'd learned in 25 years or so. "Like the army dogs?"

What beagles have to do with armies I couldn't begin to imagine. "Armies use German shepherds. Beagles are too hard to train." I could have gone on about the comic ineptitude of beagles in a K9 unit—sniffing out rodents instead of explosives, making nice to enemies proffering treats, giving away their position with uncontrollable baying—but he didn't strike me as the joking kind.

"Beagle is like bugle. Right?" We were standing by the rose beds at St. James Park. In that park I'd been asked for a number of things: the time, directions, Casey's name and openness to petting. Never etymology.

"Bugle" descends from an Old French word for "musical horn." "Beagle" is more of a conundrum. Something like it meant "small" in Celtic, "bellow" in French, "open throat" (French again) and "to scold" in German (of course: beagles are howlers). I didn't know any of this when I said, as if I had a doctorate in such matters, "They're completely different words with different roots." His eyes blazed with doubt. But one opinionated word geek deserves another, and I was the proud native speaker. If this guy wanted word talk, he'd get it. "By the way, what's your native language?"

He frowned as if I'd criticized his English. "Serbian. But I speak better English than many people here. Beagle, bugle. It's like kernel, k-e-r-n-e-l, and colonel, c-o-l-o-n-e-l."

"Don't get me wrong. Your English is perfect." His command of homonyms, not so much, but I liked his passion for the oddities of English. Let him keep his beagle and bugle. If we went down that slope like hunting dogs on the scent, there might be no end to the geek-fest. Casey had squirrels to pacify, and from his open throat there came a mighty scolding. "Sorry, we'd better move on before my dog creates a disturbance."

I met the Serb on Saturday, September 29, 2018. That day in Indonesia, an earthquake unleashed a tsunami—800 dead and counting, thousands homeless. Around the world, 50 million Facebook users learned their data had been compromised in a cyberattack. In Washington, D.C., a report from Donald Trump's administration predicted global temperatures would rise 7 degrees by 2100, but maintained that a shift away from fossil fuels was "not currently technologically feasible or economically feasible."

As things fell apart all over the globe, I discovered, a few blocks from home, that there exists a frame of mind in which beagle and bugle are connected by an effort of intellect and will. What the Serb seemed to want was to forge a little order in the world and find a place for himself in the design. The same thing I had wanted since I pictured myself in the Sailor Dog's tidy cabin. Hat on the hook for my hat, rope on the hook for my rope, pants on the hook for my pants, spyglass on the hook for my spyglass. While we were speaking, the world felt whole.

It should have happened five minutes later, or maybe the next morning. Should have slipped like a hat onto the hook of my conversation with the Serb. But this is not the way life happens. Talking with the Serb felt important because other things no longer did. Somewhere around the same time, one moment proved beyond doubt that those other things had floated out of sight. On the final leg of a walk, Casey and I passed two animated young workmates in their navy-blue presentation best, gesticulating as they strode. They had minutes left to run through the key points that would clinch or lose this deal.

I recognized these corporate players: the team leader rehearsing his boardroom body language, the striver keen to make an impression without upstaging his superior. I had been the striver once, and after a number of years (about the lifetime of a lucky dog), I became the leader. In both these roles, I let the needs of the moment push me forward, never mind that whatever consumed me might be obsolete in six months. The two men cut past me and Casey and disappeared into the press of college students on break. I wished them well with a flash of recognition that something had changed. I no longer missed working life. I felt no need for any colleague but a dog, or anything to show up for but patrol duty. This had been my Project all along. Without it, I wouldn't be keeping an eye out for JP and his Milk-Bones. I wouldn't have heard the Dead fan sing to Casey, talked etymology with the Serb. The bindweed, piercer of concrete, wouldn't be a contender for my favorite flower.

To run a magazine, I had looked out on the world and shaped a vision of it for readers. To take Casey out on patrol, I ventured into the world and let it surprise me, time after time. I wasn't just passing through. Not anymore.

Part III: Loving the World

Spring-Loaded

Things kept morphing into other things. The saplings at Corktown Common into trees, a vacant lot into empty townhouses, the builder's newly finished white boxes into homes where TVs flickered through windows and geraniums bloomed on patios. Down a laneway five minutes from home, a forgotten brick wall became a mural of a giant golden lynx. I walked Casey past just in time to see the plantings go in at its foot and snap a photo for Facebook. I wanted to commemorate that mural new and gleaming, before the taggers got to it. Another mural I loved had pretty much disappeared, one bloated tag at a time. So far, no one had messed with the lynx.

In the loveliest garden on Trinity Street, a windstorm knocked over a statuary angel. All summer she lay in two pieces—her chignoned head and torso in the dirt, her gown a jagged cup of air. Then I found her standing tall again, enfolded by her wings. The seam invisible to anyone who hadn't seen her broken.

Things that endured gave me comfort. They let me believe that endurance is the way of the world.

People still said, when Casey tried to share their lunch, "Aw, he's just a puppy."

"Puppy? He's three." Except he wasn't, not anymore. I'd lost track of time while he turned five and a half. He'd become a dog of firm opinions—less go-with-the-flow, more enough-is-enough, like a seasoned human done with people-pleasing. He lost interest in sleeping next to me, turned up his nose at late-night walks with Paul. Our Dog of Very Little Brain had acquired a new talent: divining the weather from the slant of light through our windows and the warmth (or not) of the air that seeped through the frames. Depending on his sense of the walking conditions, he'd insist on a bribe or lobby for an extra outing.

We thought we knew Casey, but we'd given ourselves too much credit. Emotionally and physically, he was ever-changing. On a routine checkup Dr. Bob got down on the floor to muss Casey's fur and offer him a treat. (Dr. Bob beats the drum for weight control but allows himself a free hand with treats.) "Whatever you're doing, keep it up," he said, one hand squeezing Casey's right foreleg. "By the way, have you noticed any limping?"

Limping? Casey tore through the dog park, leaped and spun for his dinner.

Only a vet would notice, but Dr. Bob had detected a grating he called "crepitus" (as in "decrepit"). An arthritic change, to use lay people's language. Nothing serious, just worth watching. Why did it surprise me? I was 36, not yet middle-aged, when my own right knee started giving me trouble. Then came the shoulder and the hip. Worst of all, the toe. It objected to dancing and shoes with the least hint of style. On Casey's walk it would whine ominously, as we found our rhythm, "When can we wrap this up?"

I used to think growing older was about the decline of my face. Not anymore. *Let my eyes sink into a nest of wrinkles, let me feel bad about my neck, just don't let my toe interfere with the walk. I have an active dog who needs me.* Despite the illusions of my younger years, leafy greens and two-hour workouts had failed to stop time. Instead of outgrowing those illusions, I'd transferred them to Casey. He came to us in canine adolescence when we, still thinking of ourselves as middle-aged, had just qualified for the dread label "senior." His youth magnified the joy. Now he was starting to catch up to us humans. Before we knew it, we'd be overtaken by a geezer dog with dim eyesight and a failing bladder.

That night I asked Paul, "Do you realize his life could already be half over?"

Casey had his jaws around a red squeaky ball and was giving it a noisy workout, his way of announcing it was time for the evening walk. He batted and pinned his ball like a helpless rodent.

"Oh, Casey. It's all downhill from here." I thought Paul was being playful until his expression turned reflective. "You know, I've noticed something lately. When he jumps into the car, he has to get ready. He's not as fluid as he used to be."

On Paul's next pickup at doggy day care, he chatted with a staffer whose assertive neck rubs had endeared him to Casey. "We think he's slowing down. Have you noticed?"

"Casey, slowing down? No way. He's spring-loaded."
We drank to that. *Keep running, Casey. Keep running.*

I began to watch for old people with dogs. They'd always been there, but I hadn't noticed. They don't congregate in parks, throwing balls and kibitzing and trading doggy gossip. Their dogs don't make fashion statements and are nearly always old themselves. These pairs walk the margins of the urban dogscape—the humans slump-shouldered, the dogs sway-backed, both taking it slow. They don't exactly look alike but they mirror each other, which I found just as beautiful as lithe dogs running with their people. Maybe even more so. For old pairs every outing requires tenacity and courage.

I came upon a study that sounded an alarm about old women walking dogs on leash. Our bones tend to lack the density of men's. If a dog pulls us down, we're more likely to land in the ER with a life-changing fracture. "Old women considering dog ownership must be made aware of the risk," the study cautioned. Before I grew old myself, I'd have nodded along. Now I bristle at the patronizing tone. Old women know they're not as steady on their feet as they were. They've seen hip fractures take other women down. They may or may not know about more hopeful studies linking dog ownership in old age to happier lives and deeper connections with neighbors. But they know what they cherish in a day.

When we first moved into our condo, the old woman with two little dogs used to take them out using a cane.

Later she had to grip both handles of a walker and plant each foot with care, as if positioning a rare china teacup on an unsteady table. On my way out with Casey, I would sometimes pass them inching toward the front door. The woman's pace appeared to suit the dogs, who weren't so frisky themselves, although they still had the chutzpah to growl at Casey. The trio had a route, to a local coffee shop and back.

One bright but unseasonably cold March morning, we passed them there after our ramble. My neighbor sat outside with the sun on her face, the dogs lying at her feet. I waved from across the street; she waved back, her smile beatific. A winter day with tolerable winds and no ice on the pavement is a gift to someone who can't afford to fall and lose her independence. For my neighbor every walk to the café involved some measure of risk, yet she'd made it one more day. She didn't look like a woman comparing what she had to what she'd lost. She and her dogs were folding into each other, slowing down like seasoned partners in a dance.

I'm not ready to be this woman. But I can see an older version of myself at that south-facing table, watching kids shoot hoops across the street. Casey will be licking up crumbs.

On Facebook people's dogs were dying, along with the occasional cat. Hardly a week went by without a tribute to someone's dearly missed companion. I wasn't always sure who these people were. A former colleague from the days of rubber-tablecloth lunches in Chinatown? A schoolmate last seen when Janis Joplin was flagging a ride with Bobby McGee? No matter, I read every post and took the measure of every photo. The noble Great Dane on the hiking trail, the pop-eyed pug drooling for a treat. Dogs looking out car windows, lolling on a lap beside an open book, sacked out on the lawn, spent with frolicking. The grief they left behind was running free.

The Queen buried Whisper, last of the corgis she had bred. Their bloodline went back to Susan, who rode in Her Majesty's honeymoon carriage, under a blanket. In Whisper's honor I reread *Vanity Fair*'s cover story on the corgis. The most colorful passage depicts the monarch, then in her 80s, tramping around the Scottish heath, hollering, "Keep on going!" as her dogs chase rabbits. A "rather unruly" lot, those dogs (this according to a witness). When they ran free, so did the wild streak in the woman of the sash, the tiara and the 365-day working year. Without them, who would she be?

Who would I be without Casey? I began to monitor the ages of Facebook's canine dead. *Seventeen? You had a good run, lucky dog.* My boy was years away from double digits.

Dr. Bob's clinic has two consulting rooms. We always saw him in the one on the right; I didn't know what went on behind the door on the left. I'd been waiting for advice about a sore on Casey's lip (nothing in Paul's view, a possible cancer in mine) when the lefthand door swung open to reveal a gray tabby curled up on a table. There stood

Dr. Bob, without his customary smile, and an elderly couple leaning on each other. The woman dabbed her eyes with a crumpled tissue. She seemed uncertain where to go or how to place her feet. By the time she reached Amy at the front desk, tears streaked her face.

I'd always known Amy for her laughter when Casey jumped for the treat jar. This was a different Amy, her voice not much above a whisper as she asked, "Do you need anything to take home?"

The woman looked mystified. The desk between her and Amy might as well have been a river, so far apart they seemed. It was Amy who broke the silence. "Just in case you're wondering, you don't have to pay now."

The woman said she wanted to pay. She squinted at the invoice and let out all the breath in her body. Said she didn't have that kind of money.

The man sat on one of Dr. Bob's plastic chairs with the cat's empty carrier on his lap. He had the stoic expression of someone who doesn't know what to say and fears that if he did, the effort would break him in two.

The woman put on a leopard-print coat that had seen better days. She wrapped her neck in a scarf she must have knitted herself, tugging at the ends for every inch of warmth. I told her I was sorry for her loss and had been there. Many cats of mine had died; that much was true. But I was never present when it happened. My father didn't tell me where he buried the cats hit by cars in front of Maynard Hall. He must have wanted to shield me from the awful intimacy of their dying—not in hospitals far away, like elderly relatives, but practically on our doorstep.

In my adult life Paul took over. When Casey the cat told us with his eyes that he was done, it was Paul who drove him to the vet, placed him on the table and stroked him out of this world. I didn't think our cat should be alone at the end but saw no reason for both of us to bear witness.

In Dr. Bob's waiting room, I finally understood the reason. I saw it in the slack shoulders of the man with the empty cat carrier, and on the face of his wife as she dabbed her eyes with a tissue. The cat was theirs, not his or hers. Showing up at the end was their final, shared act of love for the kitten they had brought home together on a day of hope and silliness. When a frisky young animal arrives, it's impossible not to laugh.

I said to the woman, "Your cat must have given you a lot of joy."

"She was an angel. Her name was Heidi."

If I'd been the one who left a piece of myself on a metal table, I'd want to hear Casey's name. "I'm very sorry about Heidi."

"I appreciate it, ma'am." For once I didn't mind being ma'am.

The woman's husband was heading for the door, the carrier in his hand. "Dave! Wait! Maybe we could donate the carrier. Somebody out there could use it."

Amy held out her hands for the carrier just as someone else opened the door on my right. Dr. Bob would see us now.

As Paul had predicted, the sore on Casey's lip was nothing. "Whatever you're doing, keep it, up" said Dr. Bob. Outside nothing had changed in the past half-hour. Same clump of poop on the sidewalk, same panhandler crouched outside Tim Horton's. People scurried past, shoulders hunched against the wind, as if they didn't know the world had just been repositioned on its axis.

My parents used to quote Francis Bacon: "He that hath wife and children hath given hostages to fortune." Bacon said nothing about animals.

Life Without Winter

In the first flush of love for Casey, I thought he'd make everything easier. Yet he'd made one thing immeasurably harder: a Toronto winter. Unless we found a new winter base, we'd be walking Casey through slush and blizzards. Paul and I had reached the age when falling, once a fogeyish concern, could threaten our independence. Our frisky dog had already knocked me over once, while defending us from a giant, inflatable Halloween ghost (it took two passersby to help me back up). Ice would increase the risk. We couldn't contemplate flying with Casey. Too big for the cabin, too precious for the hold. Anywhere we went, we'd have to drive. (The royal we: Paul is the family driver.) "Casey," I said, "you're a complication." My old refrain, more apt than ever.

Before Casey we could take our pick of streamlined condos in Florida—all decorated like chain hotels, few open to dogs. And yet if not for Casey we would not have found the perfect winter base, a turquoise bungalow in St. Petersburg that seemed a little big until we settled in.

The landlords, Wendy and Ed, had filled the place with art books, copper pots and well-lit reading chairs. They liked us, even gave us a shelf for belongings we'd use next winter and the one after that. We were not so much renting a house as putting down roots in the getaway home we never got around to buying, back when Florida real estate cratered and we could have made it happen. Casey slept on a couch the same color as his fur, with cushions that matched his collar. I took this for an augury of permanence. Over gulf shrimp served on Wendy's Fiestaware, we toasted our good fortune.

Our winter neighborhood wore its charm the way Diane Keaton wears a bowler hat. In the Old Northeast, I walked Casey along streets so quiet, you could hear the skitter of a leaf along the pavement. People waved to us from verandas decorated like parlors. One of the quirkier houses was for sale, with a hand-painted sign that promised:

* Florida-friendly yard
* Organic soil
* Great clothesline
* 55 windows

Casey happened to be squatting in front of this house when the occupant approached on her way home from somewhere, a lean, loose-limbed woman with a dancer's walk and flowing white hair. Before I could unroll my baggie, she bent to tell Casey, "Oh, honey! I'm so sorry to disturb your privacy." Then she floated up her front walk and disappeared into Clothesline Manor.

I'd always thought of home as a single address and its neighborhood. Home was the door we pulled our luggage through after a trip and the flick of the switch that lit up our domain. In St. Petersburg I found that home was bigger than I knew. It was every place I explored with Casey, while heading nowhere in particular. That morning, in the first bright hours after rain, we ended up at Round Lake, which is really a glorified pond. It has a fountain, a gazebo and possibly an alligator, ready to snatch a patrolling dog. I'd never seen any creature more alarming than a goose around its waters, but in Florida you can't be too careful.

I'd just found us a patch of shade far from the water when I noticed a leaf at my feet—laurel oak, one of millions that swirl and float around St. Petersburg, yet not like any other I'd seen. It held a gleaming raindrop. I still wish I had a copper bowl in the shape of that leaf, veined in deep burgundy. Not being in the market for bespoke copper art, I took a photo to share on Facebook.

If any image could express what I loved about winter in St. Pete, it was the leaf holding the raindrop as the neighborhood held its gardens, as the verandas held their wicker furniture and throw rugs, as our dog-friendly bungalow held my family.

We were in our third winter at Wendy and Ed's— cooking on their Wolf stove, watching *Grace and Frankie* on their state-of-the-art TV—when the "For Sale" sign went up. "They can't be serious," I said to Paul. "They just refurnished the den, and Wendy's been buying more Fiestaware." Wendy's crockery fixation had been a mild annoyance at first. You couldn't open a cabinet without jostling a tower of mugs or bowls that she had balanced just so. She had multiples of every color, enough to supply a coffee shop. Now I couldn't imagine a winter without that crockery and the abundance it promised.

Paul saw no reason to worry. "They're asking a lot for this part of town. Must be testing the market."

They were serious. They got their price, or close enough.

While the turquoise bungalow was ours, if only in our minds, we had strolled passed a multitude like it, with dormers and porch swings. They came in pink, yellow, seafoam green, even crimson with purple trim. But none were for rent to a family like us. The vast majority of landlords wouldn't even consider a dog, while the few pet-friendly options were already taken or way too expensive. (Wendy and Ed had been giving us a deal, not that they'd let on.) St. Pete was lost to us for next winter. Paul searched all the coastal towns in Florida, yet we were still out of luck.

As pressure mounted, Paul came up with a plan. Why not give California a try? With one driver, it would not be an easy road trip, especially in winter. Paul chose a meandering route that would dodge the worst of the weather and allow for a sightseeing break in Dallas. He had the grace not to tell me the truth: "Rona, you're a complication."

I returned Ed's copy of *Travels with Charley* to the bookshelf. Chose a tangerine mug for my last cup of coffee in the breakfast nook.

Revisiting my photo of the leaf at Round Lake, I picked up a detail I had missed. The raindrop was not resting in the leaf, but flowing out of it. What I had seen as containment was in fact a release, an emptying. The leaf couldn't hold the raindrop, any more than I could hold the small sustaining wonders of a walk with Casey.

At least LA was warm, with plenty of fine museums for the human members of the party. And it had the best dog-friendly house we could afford, which belonged to a self-proclaimed teacher of sexual and spiritual intimacy. The guru hadn't lived there for a while. (The lid to his Dutch oven turned up in the alley, the worse for wear.) The closest residential streets had more angry watchdogs than trees. With spiked collars and heavy-duty chains, the dogs barked at us behind wrought iron gates they rattled with burly shoulders. I'd never seen Casey show alarm at any dog under lock and key, but the Cujos of LA got his hackles up. They weren't going to leap those gates. I clutched the leash anyway.

Instead of Easter-egg-colored houses in our old St. Pete neighborhood, we had body shops along Pico Boulevard. Instead of Round Lake, with its fountain and gazebo, a vacant lot on Pico where Casey got a whiff of something good. Wild grass grew tall there, waving its plumes against the brilliant blue sky of a February afternoon. I let the leash go slack as Casey pushed his nose into the grass. After the snarling dogs, we'd both found respite. His a new smell, mine the unlikely beauty of this place. Perhaps I'd been too hard on LA. I should open my eyes to where I was instead of pining for where I couldn't be.

The first time Casey coughed, I didn't look down. Doesn't every dog cough now and then? He coughed again, louder. Rubbed his nose with his paw, let loose a full-bore coughing fit that shook him all over. He stretched his neck as if to force all his strength into his throat, but whatever lodged there would not be shaken loose.

"My sweet boy," I whispered, stroking his face. Fear pooled in his eyes. He felt what I saw—his running, jumping, gallivanting body held captive. I loved the ease of his body, stretched many times a day in the canine version of yoga. I often wished I could shake like Casey (a rotational stretch, in the opinion of Paul's trainer). A human must work to maintain her body; Casey *was* his body. On a normal walk we'd have been 15 minutes from the sex guru's house, but that day the walk seemed endless. Casey tottered a few paces, then coughed and gasped for breath.

The emergency clinic where we rushed him had bigger windows and brighter decor than any place that had treated our human emergencies. Purposeful cheer radiated from everyone we met on our pilgrimage from front desk to inner sanctum. They asked Paul to carry him there lest other waiting animals catch his cough. I'd never seen Casey in Paul's arms before, head dangling and front paws akimbo, but then Casey had never been touched by anything that looked this dire. We sat on hard chairs with Casey hacking at our feet, waiting for deliverance from evil.

Dr. Cynthia Bertram listened to my story of the grass and the coughing fit. Then she told us treating Casey wasn't going to be simple. From my description of the grass, she concluded he'd been sniffing foxtails. They have sharp seeds, each one with an awn engineered by nature to drive the seed forward. Once inhaled by a curious animal, the seed and its awn only move one way—deeper into the animal's body, where it might penetrate a lung, the stomach, the brain, any organ at all.

I'd never heard of foxtails. The dog people I knew in LA, my two nephews and a friend, never warned, "Make sure Casey doesn't sniff any foxtails." My mind began to reel, but Dr. Bertram wasn't done. The awns would not degrade in the body. She had seen infections, some of them fatal.

"I don't mean to alarm you," said Dr. Bertram with practiced neutrality. "These are worst-case scenarios." She recommended an immediate rhinoscopy to hunt out the awn and flush his nostrils. Until she looked inside, she couldn't say where the awn might be lurking, how many twists and turns the search would take, or what her efforts might cost. The rhinoscopy alone would be $2,500.

This was her idea of not meaning to alarm?

She did mention one other reason Casey might be coughing—an allergic reaction we could treat with an over-the-counter antihistamine. That was less likely, in her view. And the longer we delayed the rhinoscopy, the greater the risk of potentially lethal damage. "I realize this is a lot for you to take in. So I'll give you some time to consider your options."

Casey lay on the floor in his let's-get-moving posture, head between paws. His cough had subsided a little, but Dr. Bertram's diagnosis chilled me. On a typical afternoon in LA, I'd be deciding which tacos to order at the funky little place around the corner. Planning our visit to the Caravaggio exhibition at the Getty. Now all I wanted was more of what we had with Casey—the click and the jingle, the bark and the snore, the coiled warmth between us at the end of the day.

Paul put his hand on mine. "You want to spend the money, don't you?"

"There are no guarantees," Dr. Bertram had told us, her way of saying the potentially lethal foxtail awn might elude her. Perhaps it had never been there at all. But I was mad about our dog and wanted him well. If spending the money boosted our odds even slightly, I'd do it. I knew Paul loved Casey just as much as I did. Loved him on sight in Liz's foyer, while I was still asking myself, "Can we do better?"

"Let's try the antihistamine first," Paul said. "If Casey doesn't respond, we can always bring him back here." I swallowed hard. In a crisis my husband makes a plan while I worry. This plan made sense. On our way to the drugstore, we stopped at a park with sweeping views of the city and let Casey poke his nose into the plants along the trail. Grasses that might have been foxtails swayed in the distance. From this vantage point, in this company, you wouldn't know the snarling dogs existed. Everything shimmered in the setting sun.

If we ever went back to LA, it wouldn't be on a road trip with Casey. My only souvenir of the city was a foxtail from the vacant lot. I taped it to a piece of notepaper, along with an awn that resembled the setting for a ring, claw-like prongs that have lost their stone. By this time, I'd read up on foxtails. An awn can burrow for years inside a dog before the animal falls desperately ill. Or it can leave vital organs alone and turn up in an autopsy. I had no idea where Casey's awn was lurking, or if it even existed. I told myself the antihistamines had worked, but Casey could still be in trouble. The vets most skilled at foxtail emergencies have practiced out west, prime territory for the plant. Dr. Bob was not among them. "I've heard of these things," he said. "Let's wait and see."

I pinned the souvenir to my bulletin board, where for months I watched it dry out between an old *New Yorker* cartoon and my favorite photo of my sister and me. One day I noticed it was gone.

Lost and Found

We no longer fantasized about a trip to Monet's garden at Giverny. Wendy and Ed's turquoise house, with its scratched floorboards and bathroom window that refused to open, had become our lost kingdom. The minor imperfections of the place underscored the allure of everything else. The house didn't tantalize our senses or stretch our mental horizons, but that was the point. It soothed and cosseted. Behind its double doors with the matching floral wreaths, we could let our complications go.

Along with the house, we missed the neighborhood coffee shop where you could sip your brew of choice in a vintage theater seat from the days of Greta Garbo. We missed watching for dolphins along Tampa Bay while Casey got acquainted with the local dogs. And although I can't speak for Paul, I missed my chance encounters with St. Pete dog folk. Casey wouldn't be Casey if he didn't introduce me to men. We met a few on our rambles, and they couldn't have been more different from the poor cowboys of Toronto.

In the soft light of early evening, the two of us approached a brick bungalow that stood out in this genteel part of town like paper plates at a Junior League tea party. Odds and sods of plastic furniture, not all of it upright, were strewn about the lawn. On a table sat what looked to be the dregs of a yard sale. Beside it stood a ringer for Steve Buscemi in loser mode. He was talking to his dogs, a peppy Chihuahua who took a shine to Casey, and a pit bull mix with malevolent eyes. I listened for their names, Taco and Pirate.

Chihuahuas are the one small breed that Casey deems worthy of notice. As he offered his hind end to genial Taco, Pirate the pit bull got his hackles up. I'd have to keep an eye on Casey or things could get ugly.

Music drifted from the house. The Buscemi ringer yelled, "Hey! You like Stevie Ray Vaughan?"

I didn't know Stevie Ray Vaughan from Stevie Nicks. "Not sure. Why don't you hum me some Stevie Ray Vaughan?"

This didn't win me any points with him, but neither did it knock me off his prospect list. He had the twinkly eyes of a man who believes he is charming, if years away from hot. "Stevie Ray Vaughan's a jazz guitarist."

While I steeped in my ignorance, his buddy shuffled out of the house. Big guy with a paunch some decades in the making and a gray bird's nest of a beard. Baggy shorts exposed the knotted veins in his legs. Thirty years ago he must have resembled Jeff Bridges in *The Big Lebowski*, but in his current state he made The Dude look like Prince Harry. He took his sweet time getting to the curb. "You know Ida Lupino?"

"Of course." Here I was on firmer ground. After school Joyce and I used to watch old movies on TV. I vaguely remembered seeing Ida Lupino's name in credits, in that swirly '40s script. She had sultry eyes and a dangerous manner. Ida Lupino wouldn't take any guff.

"Here's the thing about Ida Lupino. Nobody remembers anymore. In her day she was bigger than Katharine Hepburn."

How much of what The Dude said had any connection to the truth? I thought I'd drift a while on the current of his rambling. His expression turned languorous. "You know about Ida Lupino's brother?"

Pirate had begun to snarl. He stared at Casey as if working on a plan. While the Buscemi clone held him by the collar, Pirate dug his paws into the ground and pulled. I drew Casey closer. Laurie had a rule for challenging situations: Move on. But I wasn't ready to move. I was too busy thinking about Ida Lupino's brother. The Dude had me stumped. "She had a brother?"

"Sure did. Her brother Hal."

Buscemi gripped Pirate's collar with both hands. "You two better wrap this up 'cause I can't hold him much longer!"

Buscemi had a point, but any second I'd remember this brother. If I said his name, rolled it on my tongue, it would come to me. "Hal Lu . . ."

The Dude laughed until his belly shook. "Gotcha there! Jalapeno! None of the ladies see that coming!"

Back at my computer, I Google-checked the conversation. Stevie Ray Vaughan played blues, not jazz. Ida Lupino made her name as an actress but her breakthrough as a director, all but unheard-of for a woman of her time. If she had a brother, I found no mention of him. Those pranksters would say anything for a laugh, but I had to hand it to them: They showed me a good time. In their eyes I was not the kind of woman who'd correct a fellow's grammar, just one of the ladies who'd let him treat her to a Miller and fall for his joke. I'd play that role again, if I got the chance.

At the thought of a second winter without the comforts of St. Pete, I made a last-ditch attempt to recapture the lost kingdom. By searching the rental sites a year in advance, I could beat the competition and snag the ideal spot. Perhaps the new owners of the turquoise house were going to spend the winter somewhere else. For tenants endorsed by Wendy and Ed, they might cut us the deal of the season. I dared to hope. But what I found—the only real possibility—was a bungalow around the corner from our lost kingdom. Same price, a fair bit smaller.

It belonged to Barry, a musician about town. His tenants all agreed you couldn't rent from a more helpful guy. I studied the photos on Airbnb. He didn't seem to own much by way of tables and chairs, but he displayed an impressive collection of instruments: bass, trombone, ukulele, guitar. An upright piano occupied the spot where less freewheeling types would have placed a dining room table. Top marks for originality, though. Where else would you find a fridge with guitar necks for door handles?

While not quite what we had in mind, Barry's house would give us access to the kingdom's outer reaches—the dog park where Casey liked to pee through the fence, the bayside walk that offered some fresh discovery every morning. If not a catamaran race, then the trainees from Southwestern Guide Dogs, honing the art of ignoring rascals like Casey. I might even have another confab with Buscemi and The Dude. "It's a step down from Wendy and Ed's," Paul said before I could say so myself, "but let's take it."

Casey always knows when we're not on the highway anymore. He can tell by the sound of the engine and the lurch at a stoplight that we've almost reached his new domain. Sniffing must be done, boundaries enforced. By the time we arrived at Barry's, he'd pulled himself erect— ears back, muzzle high. Whatever was soon to happen, it had to be about him.

"Do you think he'll try to go back to Wendy and Ed's?" I asked Paul (to us the house would never be anything else). We both agreed I should lose no time leading Casey past his former home. If the new owners happened to be puttering about, I'd chat them up, share some memories. Just because they hadn't put the place up for rent didn't mean they wouldn't rent it to people who'd care for that fine-boned house as if it were their own.

Barry's house didn't have the finest bones, but he'd painstakingly fixed it up himself and hung art by his friends on the walls. As he gave us the tour, I said, "It looks exactly like the photos on the website." I'd read enough online reviews to know that "not as nice as the web page" is a killer. The real rap on Barry's place was "not as nice as Wendy and Ed's." But I liked Barry, in part because Casey did. They were making friends, with much licking and leaping on Casey's part, while I made invidious comparisons. If Paul and I had a son eking out a living as a musician, he might be a lot like this fellow in a fedora, baggy shorts and wild socks designed to sag at the ankles.

Our musician son, like Barry, might have a kitchen counter made of distressed concrete, dappled with the outline of every wine glass and coffee spill to land there. Since Barry had neither a proper table nor any semblance of a desk, we'd be doing it all at that counter—my writing, Paul's genealogy projects, the cooking, the bills. At Wendy and Ed's we had two work stations. "Anything you need, give me a shout," said Barry. "My place is on top of the garage. I want you two to enjoy yourselves." He paused to give Casey one more scratch. "And I'd be happy to look after this guy if you're ever stuck. Just ask."

That evening I walked Casey past the lost kingdom. We approached as a gray-haired woman lugged a Christmas tree out the door. She didn't look up while I checked on the house. Still turquoise, thank goodness, with the porch swing still in its familiar spot. The new people loved the house—that was clear from the freshly watered garden with its perky if prim impatiens. Wendy and Ed had let the yard get a little scruffy, but they would not have chosen the current lawn statuary, grinning frogs and cavorting children. From my vantage point across the street, I couldn't see much of the interior except the staid pale-blue paint that had replaced the exuberant crimson and marigold.

I waited for Casey to pull me to the door, he waited for me to get on with his walk. For all he cared, we could have been loitering in front of CVS. He'd already made himself at home at Barry's.

I'd just cleared away the remains of dinner when something came over Casey, an intimation of trouble he alone could set right. It lurked in the primary bathroom, at the foot of the linen closet. There Casey stood on alert—head cocked, tail rigid, nose twitching. At times he let out a faint whimper. Whatever he detected both distressed and enthralled him. He would shuffle away to his bed but agitation kept pulling him back to his post. So it continued all night, fitful sleep interspersed with reconnaissance trips to the bathroom. I only knew this because Paul observed it in the course of his own fitful night. "Casey has found a nocturnal hobby," he said. For once Casey didn't respond to his name. His efforts had worn him out.

Paul is an expert on nocturnal hobbies. While I sleep, he solves puzzles or reflects on genealogical problems. Breakfast time for me is often bedtime for him. Whatever Casey had found, it was turning him into Paul's twitchy companion of the dark. Casey knew something had to be alive in that bathroom, and he would not rest until he had dispatched it.

Did Barry know anything about this critter? He suspected a possum. "Think I heard one poking around myself a few times. I hope it's not bothering you." No, only

Casey was bothered. He kept vigil all night, then barely opened an eye until mid-morning.

"I think he preferred the other house," Paul said. A case of projection, I thought. He'd recently called my attention to the lack of good reading spots at Barry's.

The other house had five (six if you counted the porch swing). But it didn't have a possum. Casey had embarked on a quest, like a mathematician homing in on a proof, or a poet obsessed by an elusive line. Nature had given him the nose and claws of a hunter. Maybe here he could finally accomplish what he was born to do.

If Casey had ever made a kill, I couldn't imagine where it had happened. Surely not at the prison or the shelter. At the doggy farm where he boarded, entire days of tearing around hadn't netted him a single critter. "The squirrels love to tease him," said his friend Whitney, who ran the place. Based on the evidence to date, Casey had as much flair for hunting as The Dude had with women. All enthusiasm, no finesse.

Yet Casey threw himself into failure with every expectation of success, and I loved his happy ineptitude. On our walks he seemed to forget the leash, jumping for squirrels as if nothing stopped him. For Casey any moment outdoors held the possibility of triumph.

Days had passed since Casey last kept watch in Barry's primary bathroom. I thought the possum must have moved on, like mice deterred by the scent of a cat. The possum had moved, alright. But not far. One night as Paul opened the kitchen door, Casey bolted into a tunnel-like alley from which neither fish-skin treats nor a chunk of cheddar cheese could entice him. If he'd found a crawl-space, he could hide out there for hours while we flailed and cajoled.

Worse, he might take off in pursuit of a scent and end up who knew where. Faded lost-dog posters flashed before my eyes: "Needs his medication." "My little girl's best friend." Tomás, the canine ghost of our neighborhood in Mexico City: "Please help me bring him home." How many of those dogs ever made it back to the people who loved them? While I pictured Casey's amber eyes on a poster, Paul fumbled for his phone, the closest thing we had to a flashlight. The beam found Casey in the darkest corner of the alley, jaws around the throat of the possum. The narrow alley could accommodate only one human, so I let Paul pry the two apart.

Once he'd dragged Casey inside, to whimper and sniff at the kitchen door, I asked Paul what had become of the possum. Still out there, he said. Not moving. "They play dead, you know."

I knew, I just didn't believe it. If Paul was right, then Casey had failed in his mission. And I wanted success for Casey. I was hoping for a clean, swift kill, not an agonizing death from mortal wounds, followed by odiferous decay in some unreachable cranny. When Paul checked on the possum a few hours later, he found it sitting up, bright-eyed and cool as could be. Next morning it was gone.

We'd just booked our next winter stay at Barry's, and some of us had unfinished business. Casey still gave the bathroom baseboards the occasional dispirited sniff, muttering under his breath. Whatever lurked there had better not get too comfortable. The Terminator would be back next winter. As for me, I still hadn't reconnected with The Dude, whose house I'd ambled past on any number of walks with Casey. Far as I could tell, he still lived there. The plastic tub chairs had barely moved. The table sported its familiar jumble of unrecognizable objects. But I saw no living creature, human or canine. I didn't miss Pirate, but Taco was the second-best dog in the world, and I never got to ask him "Who's a good boy?"

On our last walk that way, I noticed a change. Someone had pulled a tub chair to the near edge of the yard and heaped it with star fruit for the taking. More fruit hung from every branch of the tree overhead, a touch of beauty I had missed until that moment. I'd have picked up a star fruit if not for Casey's leash and my purse and how far we still had to go.

A Can of Birds

One morning just after school let out for the summer, I stopped with Casey in the churchyard at Little Trinity. The forecast had promised a heat wave but for now a fresh breeze tossed the maples. Casey had his snout buried in a patch of grass. Of all the lush green spots he might have chosen that day, it was this one that sang to his scent receptors. He angled his hind end over the most pungent sprig and blessed it with a shower of pee, letting a few drops land on his leg.

The air was soft, the lawn that tender green that's gone by mid-July, my head full of grief. The space between my eyes felt like the Hoover Dam holding back a Colorado River of tears. I recognized this feeling. It had stopped the world when my mother died, and again when I lost my friend Val.

I used to think that only a beloved face and voice could unleash it, but this time I was mourning an entire country—my native country—in Donald Trump's presidency. I couldn't keep track of the assaults on liberty and justice. Yeats clanged in my head: "The ceremony of innocence is drowned; The best lack all conviction while the worst/ Are full of passionate intensity." When I reached for my phone to check the news, paragraphs blurred and seethed. "You're reading too much of that stuff," Paul would say. "Don't you see it's a toxic habit?"

I'd made a promise to myself: no headline checks on Casey's walk. This hour was supposed to be my haven from despair, but the weight of the phone had been making my fingers twitch. It thumped against my hip as we walked, brushed my hand as I reached for one of Casey's dried sardines. It whispered to me the way hidden bottles of vodka must have whispered to my father. I no longer believed in news of deliverance, only in the certainty of a lower low, a darker dark than seemed possible only yesterday. I had to stay abreast of how low, how dark, how far beyond my power to make a difference. Every day I broke my promise to keep my hands off the phone. Casey sniffed, I scrolled.

We had the churchyard to ourselves. Even the squirrels had gone quiet, leaving Casey to pursue his olfactory pleasures and me to feel the weight of my sorrow. When the first tear slid down my cheek, I didn't brush it away. The leash trembled in my hand, Casey's way of saying, "Here I am."

If she were with me, Val would have had a wise and pithy comment on the state of the world. She would ground me with the brave, biting wit that was inseparable from her kindness. When Val skewered cruelty, the one thing she abhorred, she affirmed her faith that good would come through in the end, tattered but dauntless. A few minutes of Val would set me right; I wasn't asking for that hike we never got around to taking. But first I'd have to bring her up to speed. Val died the year Barack Obama was elected. Now every headline was a wave carrying her further into the past.

The closest I ever came to joining a church was a 12-step meeting in the basement of one. Val had persuaded me to go and took time off work to sit beside me on a folding chair the first time. I struggled to get past Step One, turning my life and my will over to the care of God as I understood him. No deities for me, least of all a male one. Val said God could be whatever I believed in that was greater than myself, but the problem stumped me and I didn't stay long in the group. Many years later I had finally settled on the answer: kindness. The trampling of it cut deep.

Little Trinity is my neighborhood's oldest church and the most welcoming to the eye. The spires at St. James Cathedral soar higher than Little Trinity's modest brick tower, but whoever designed this church in the heyday of Gothic Revival didn't want to intimidate its first parishioners, Irish refugees from the potato famine. The only architectural adornments are three botanical flourishes above the portals, but I wouldn't call it dour. Little Trinity combines grace with solidity, aspiration with awareness of the earthbound. The church sits in the shade of a towering maple, its leaves streaked with blight but still the neighborhood's loveliest tree. On warm Sundays guitar music drifts from the open lancet windows, soft enough not to wake any homeless person sleeping on a bench outside.

The last time Casey and I stopped at Little Trinity, we met the guiding spirit behind a child-size herb garden, recently planted by grownups down on their luck. Their supervisor gave me the lowdown while scratching Casey's butt. He worked at the addiction clinic around the corner; the gardeners were his clients. "They're all in recovery, most of them doing well. The ones that aren't doing well I see three times a day."

Weeks had passed since that conversation, but the lone rhubarb plant was no taller and the basil had just enough leaves for two servings of caprese salad. I noted one sage plant, a ruffle of curly parsley. At the rate this garden was going, there wouldn't be much of a harvest, but the gardeners had aced their weeding. The earth looked moist and loose, a fine bed for worms. When Casey lifted his leg above the garden, I pulled him away just in time.

We happened to be facing Church House, where kids attend Sunday school. I had stood with Casey on that very spot many times, seeing nothing but a weathered brick wall. This time my eye fell on the window ledge where someone had placed a red paint can, turned sideways, a clump of dried grass protruding from one end. A sign said, in red Magic Marker, "Please, please, don't touch or come near. Trying to save babies and nest. Thank you!"

Birds too young or too broken to fly are the only ones Casey has ever come close to mauling. I tightened the leash, then drew just close enough to snap a photo. Whoever was saving the nest had taken a stand for kindness, the first good news of the day. That person didn't listen to the inner voice that asks, "Why bother? What if this doesn't work?"

The King streetcar clattered past. Voices shouted things I couldn't make out. I was listening to the voice in my mind, Emily Dickinson's, and everything else fell away:

> *If I can stop one heart from breaking,*
> *I shall not live in vain;*
> *If I can ease one life the aching,*
> *Or cool one pain,*
> *Or help one fainting robin*
> *Unto his nest again,*
> *I shall not live in vain.*

I hadn't thought of this poem since middle school. Mrs. Wilcox read it to our class with the diction of an elocutionist and the bearing of Margaret Dumont in *A Night at the Opera*. Her silhouette hinted of a close encounter between a full figure and a corset. Any poem she esteemed I disdained on principle. Fainting robin? Get the smelling salts! Yet Dickinson's poem still found a place in my memory and lodged there like a lucky stone at the bottom of a deep pocket. That day at Little Trinity Church, it was there for me. It came to me in snatches, with Google filling in what I couldn't recall. This time my phone was a lifeline, not the path to despair. Whoever positioned the can of birds would appreciate that poem.

Casey's four feet and my two beat a comforting rhythm on the sidewalk. All the way home I wondered who was rescuing birds. I didn't expect to know who built Stonehenge or painted the caves at Lascaux. Those people lived and died in unimaginably distant times. But someone in my own neighborhood cared enough to turn an empty paint can into a bird sanctuary. I had a candidate in mind. I'd seen her more than once cleaning up the church yard, a lean woman with tattooed arms and a blond topknot.

I pictured her bending over the fallen nestlings. What could she do? She thought of the empty paint can. Just the thing. She didn't know if the birds would pull through, any more than Emily Dickinson, writing alone with scarcely any readers, knew if her fainting robin would be remembered. But the bird rescuer got her piece of cardboard and her red Magic Marker. She stepped back and looked at her call to anyone passing by. "Trying to save babies and nest." She'd underlined "save" twice so no one who looked up would miss the point. Yes, it would do.

Summer that year was hot and bright. By August the Magic Marker had faded from red to pink, although the can still sat on the window ledge. From time to time I saw the bird rescuer at work. Her determined stride and air of intense concentration made me hesitate to approach her. Asking this woman what became of the birds would not be like cheering on a muralist or a groundskeeper at the park. Those people were doing what they set out to do; the bird rescuer might have failed in a mission close to her heart. It worried me that she hadn't moved the can, and I didn't want to raise a painful subject with a stranger. At last I couldn't keep the question to myself any longer.

The woman's eyes grew misty. "They all died. But I'm going to try again next year."

She bent to stroke Casey as we thanked each other—her for trying to save the birds, me for watching and caring. What we held between ourselves was not failure but hope.

I cultivated a new habit: watching for brokenness I could mend. The bad news didn't let up, but it pained me less when I tended my corner of the world. If the bird rescuer could do it, I could do it too. On Casey's walk I rescued lost things—a dog's tag on the street, a cell phone on the pavement, a pair of tortoiseshell sunglasses on the grass at St. James Park, where someone must have lain to feel the sun on her eyelids. The tag and the phone I managed to return to the owners. The sunglasses, last time I checked, still languished in the lost and found at St. James Cathedral, but two out of three seemed a respectable score. Once per walk, twice when I was feeling energetic, I bent to pick up so-called orphan poop—turds left behind by heedless dog folk. The slackers angered me less when I made a small corrective gesture. Some dogs took extravagantly formless dumps, but I'd tackled worse the day Casey met Adrian. By picking up challenging orphans, I sharpened my appreciation for Casey's sleek offerings. Who'd have thought I walked the Brâncuși of poop?

Maybe orphan pickup would catch on. Imagine the difference if other dog walkers stepped up. No more rank smears on the bottom of our shoes, less bacteria in our water, healthier streams and ponds. I became ostentatious about my crusade, every scoop a call to arms. In a woman resting with her dog on a bench, I detected a likely recruit. Let this woman see how committed I was.

She didn't burst out laughing; it was more of a chuckle. "Look behind you! While you were opening the bag, your dog did his business."

Good grief, so he had. In my zeal, I hadn't noticed.

Water for Michael

Between an overpass and a Lincoln dealership sits the little courtyard known as Percy Park. I didn't know it was there until Casey peed against the arbor at its edge. A stone path led us to a garden where morning glories climbed and allium burst from planters. I came to think of Percy Park as our private retreat, where on walk after walk we never met a soul. But all along wanderers had been camping there, leaving piles of trash—cast-off clothes, empty bottles, food wrappers and overstuffed bags disgorging more of the same.

That's where I met him, a man of indeterminate age with hollows in his cheeks and a utility broom in his hand. Not your average poor cowboy, although he had that look. He wanted me to know he was taking care of the mess. "Disgusting," he muttered. "Why do people do this to the park?" He reminded me a little of myself in a self-righteous mood. He didn't ask to pet Casey, but the presence of a dog seemed to make me someone he could trust. "I'm Michael, by the way."

"I'm Rona. And this is Casey Charles Jones."

"Michael John McLean." When he smiled, I saw his missing teeth.

Anyone can visit Percy Park, but it's a shared backyard for those who live in the renovated workers' cottages on Percy Street. On warm Sundays Casey and I have sometimes threaded our way around a neighborhood yoga class in the park. "Do you live here?" I asked, already knowing the answer. The residents of Percy Street don't have blank spaces in their mouths or wear jeans untouched by Tide.

Michael leaned on his broom. "My daughter died nine years ago. Brain cancer. Only 13. I hit a bad patch. Lost my job, lost my wife. Since then I've been living on the street. I'm on social assistance, but I never ask for money. I like to clean up places like this. It's my way of giving back."

He told me about his daughter. How gentle she was, how smart. When the doctors discovered the cancer, they gave her 11 months—exactly the time she had, and it couldn't have been more terrible. He watched her suffer through the chemo, which the doctors knew wouldn't help but recommended anyway because they had nothing else to offer.

Michael's eyes had reddened as he spoke. I didn't see any tears but I could sense them pressing against his eye sockets. He'd been a handsome man, still was if you looked closely.

I told him how sorry I was about his daughter. Thanked him for cleaning up a park on my walking route.

"Could you do one thing for me?" he asked. I thought it would be small, and it was. He handed me a plastic water bottle. "If you could fill this for me, I'd be grateful."

"Glad to. There are water fountains where we're going, at Corktown Common. It's beautiful there."

I'd become an evangelist for Corktown Common, a newish park that deserved to be a city-wide destination but still felt like a neighborhood secret. Where brownfields used to be, walkers can now wander a prairie, listen to frogs in a marsh, climb a hillock that looks as if it's been there forever but in fact was designed, like the rest of the park. I nattered a bit about green design (native plants, recycled storm water), and Michael told me he'd go to Corktown Common himself.

Once he knew how to find the fountain, he could fill his bottle there anytime. He wouldn't need to ask for anyone's help. And I wouldn't need to return to Percy Park instead of heading straight home, an increasingly attractive idea. My feet ached; the day was heating up. I was not the kind of person who adds 20 minutes to her walk just to fill someone's water bottle, much as I liked to think otherwise. I told Michael he'd love Corktown Common. Hoped I was doing him a different kind of favor.

The fountain where I sent Michael is next to a splashpad where Paul and I like to take our younger grandson. That day it rang with children's voices. Every rock had become a perch for a family with towels and plastic buckets. Kids leaped in the spray, parents took photos. I pictured Michael arriving there, remembering his daughter at splash-pad age, and her mother beside him on a beach towel. Once he too had a family. Nine years ago, ten if you count the year of cancer that tore his family apart. I thought of something he'd told me. "People judge me because I'm dirty and thin.

They can tell I'm on the street." People like the parents at the splash pad. They wouldn't want Michael anywhere near their kids, would never guess he used to be one of them.

If Michael got to Corktown Common, his heart would sink. For 20 minutes of my time, I could have spared him that.

He liked to clean up parks, I frequented a few. Surely I'd have a chance to set things right between us. "I've been thinking about your daughter," I would say, not to be kind but because it was the truth. "What was her name?" I kept an eye on his corner at Percy Park, but he never reappeared. Trash did, for a while. A ripped suitcase, an abandoned computer. Poor cowboys like Michael don't lug computers around. It wasn't just wanderers who'd been treating the park like a dump. The worst offenders must have had closets and basements.

Someone eventually restored the park to a condition Michael would approve, although he might never see it again. I would have other chances to do the right thing. But not for him. He would not remember me as the woman I wanted to be.

I had a question for my sister. No one else would know the answer. "When we were growing up, were we ever taught to be kind?"

Joyce recalled no such thing. We were taught to be creative and ambitious, to rise above others instead of walking beside them. We learned to write thank-you notes and speak when spoken to, but only to avoid embarrassing our parents. "Do unto others" never came up. This had never struck me as odd until I started meeting people with Casey. Now it staggered me how simple it was to make someone's day. How natural, but not for me.

The thought was new, and yet I recognized the feeling. It was like that stage in a yoga practice where a stiff joint begins to move for the first time in memory—a sensation that a teacher of mine called "joy pain." A great deal of quivering precedes the letting go. The downside of a shoulder that fulfills its purpose at last is wondering how you ever managed without one. I had somehow spent a lifetime in a stiff heart that was finally beginning to expand.

I remembered that strange dream I had after we adopted Casey. The wetsuit I had on, the almost-lover with his teeth on the zipper. My husband called it: That was no man, that was Casey.

What Jesus Said

Before Casey, I never went anywhere without a purse big enough to hold a paperback book and a collapsible umbrella. Things I needed got lost amid crumpled ticket stubs, loose ibuprofen tablets and an emery board on its last legs. When the thing you need this minute is a poop bag, you don't want to be rooting around. So instead of the purse, I started carrying the slim nylon pouch that holds my dog-walking kit. Not the whole kit, just the parts I have to reach with one hand—phone, keys, treats, the all-important bags. The rest of the kit is in my head, bits and bobs of poetry. There aren't many poems I know from start to finish; sometimes all I remember is a mood. After my encounter with Michael, I often thought of a poem steeped in loneliness, "Chemin de Fer" by Elizabeth Bishop.

In one stanza clean as a bone, Bishop tells a story of two lost souls, an agitated narrator out for a walk and a hermit in the distance. The pond between them is a burial ground for grudges. The narrator sees the hermit; it's not clear if he can see her. She hears him scream that love should be

235

put into action. Who could argue with that? Some poets would frame the sentiment as their own hard-won wisdom, but Elizabeth Bishop takes no pity on the reader or herself. She aims to unsettle, not to console. And so she gives the poem's great truth to a desperate and powerless man who doesn't know if anyone hears him. Only an echo replies.

The narrator could be me, the hermit any poor cowboy I've met with Casey. The hermit knows what it takes to escape from aloneness, but he's run out of hope. Something tells me Bishop had too. An alcoholic with a history of tortured relationships, she could have been describing her own inner landscape.

Suppose I tried putting love into action. I knew this would be an honorable mission. I didn't know what it would mean for me as a citizen of the neighborhood I'd come to know with Casey. Never thought, *Today's the day I find out.*

That day I only meant to celebrate the rightness of the morning. Sundress weather for walking Casey, a new friend made along the way. A killer aquafit class had left me flushed and hungry. I was craving a double scoop of Ed's burnt marshmallow ice cream. If the Queen streetcar didn't let me down, I'd beat the morning rush.

The streetcar gods were with me. Sunlight warmed my shoulder. I was halfway into a daydream when a loud male voice pulled me back, preaching holy war in Jesus's name. Muslims were killers, he said. Blood sacrifice was their mission. The preacher sat a few rows behind me—hard eyes flashing, cheeks plump with baby fat. Across the aisle a brown-skinned woman in a niqab pressed her cheek against the window. People looked at their phones, their hands, the passing scene. A woman with a careworn face muttered under her breath while heaving a shopping cart onto the street. As the doors banged shut behind her, I saw the calculation she had made. She wouldn't miss her stop for this affair. Let someone else respond.

Why not me?

The streetcar rattled east toward Ed's. The woman in the niqab hadn't moved; her eyes glistened. The holy warrior was spitting blood. I had never been the one who calls out hatred. Never defied an angry male stranger. Mr. F-Bomb had trampled all over me that winter day in the dog park, but damned if I'd let this punk trample the woman in the niqab. I stood and faced the holy warrior. "It's time for you to stop. I've had enough and the rest of us have too." Of course they'd had enough. How could it be otherwise?

The holy warrior sneered. "You're a hypocrite. I have a right to free speech. You're interrupting our conversation."

"Conversation? You're not having a conversation. You're abusing someone with your monologue."

He sat with his bony knees splayed, his bare arms folded across his chest. The posture of the class wise guy who's just been challenged by the teacher and is waiting to face the higher authority in the office. "Well, then, you're interrupting my monologue. You should sit down. Jesus said, 'Mind your own business.'"

So the world was his toy and Jesus his most prized action figure. The nerve. "Jesus said nothing of the kind."

"Sure did. Three times."

I haven't read the New Testament since I studied the Bible as literature. Rocking with the motion of the streetcar, I thought of what Jesus really said, the one thing I could quote without checking the virtual King James Bible. The holy warrior needed to hear it. "Jesus said, 'Love one another.' Buster, I don't see any love from you."

I'd never called anyone "buster" before. How pleasingly it rolled off my tongue. Surely it would inspire someone to back me up. Of the dozen or so passengers, I only needed one to shift the balance between me and the holy warrior. There they sat, looking anywhere but at the two of us. Minding their own business, as people do in public confrontations. I was on my own and out of words; the holy warrior was still on a tear. The Muslim woman had her hand against the veiled contours of her lips. Maybe I should have sat down beside her, murmuring reassurance, but it wasn't clear she understood English or would find my presence any comfort. I turned my back to the holy warrior and strode to the door with his venom ringing in my ears.

All I'd asked of my excursion was a double scoop of burnt marshmallow. I wasn't planning to defend anyone. In a Muskoka chair outside Ed's, my ice cream softened by the sun, I took stock of the difference I had made. Not much, as far as I could tell. The Muslim woman knew one person had her back, but the holy warrior thought he'd won. My fellow passengers might think of me someday. In the thick of a blast of hatred, they might ask themselves,

"Why not me?" But they might just as easily conclude, "It's not worth it. Soon this will all be over."

For me there was no such thing as "over." I still asked myself why I hadn't filled Michael's water bottle or stood up to the F-bomber. In close to 50 years' experience of adult life, you'd think a person could acquire some gumption, but I took cover behind the magazine page, the podium or the screen. I thought this would always be so until I started walking a dog and began to feel responsible for the spirit and cohesiveness of my neighborhood.

When I led a team at work, I was judged on my results. I had "deliverables" and "KRAs"—terms that irked me but reassured me too. I never had to ask "How am I doing?" I had targets, and I met or surpassed them. Now I was more like the bird rescuer. I'd never know if my stand had made a difference to anyone other than myself.

I didn't expect to see the holy warrior again. I trusted the city to swallow him up. One hot Sunday morning in July, I led Casey down a shady street to give his paws a break. Wind chimes tinkled on front porches. Anyone who crossed our path would be taking it slow—nursing an iced latte from the coffee shop facing the parkette, shooting the breeze with a neighbor.

The bare-chested man stood out for the rush he was in. He cut in front of us with a bag of garbage, dumped it into the bin. Looked up and through me. I remembered those hard, cold eyes and the softness of his choirboy cheeks. I gripped Casey's leash as a shiver went through me. An old woman expects to be ignored by a young man in a hurry, but this old dame had given him hell.

Furious men must live somewhere. This one lived around the corner from the Queen streetcar line. We'd been near his stop when I heard him light into the Muslim woman, and we might share a streetcar again. The holy warrior was my neighbor.

Jesus said, "Love thy neighbor as thyself." This according to Matthew, whose story Caravaggio told in the frescoes that drew me to his art. When Matthew heard the call from Jesus, he didn't love his neighbors. He was counting the money he'd collected from them. He saw the light and turned his back on darkness. I'd seen thunderbolt transformations in so many legends and stories, I forgot real life is different. In real life, darkness keeps tugging you back. There were neighbors I could love for the way they shared our common spaces. But not the holy warrior.

I hated him.

Missing

You never know what you might learn in a condo elevator when you have a dog in tow. Between the ground floor and ours, I got talking rescue dogs and their quirks with a man who said, "My daughter and her wife have a rescue who's terrified of electric wheelchairs."

I'm still pleasantly surprised to hear anyone say "my daughter and her wife," but I did a double take at the mention of a canine wheelchair phobia. Thunder and fireworks, absolutely. A mouse, a stuffed lamb, a kitten and a Roomba all terrify certain dogs I've seen online. But wheelchairs? "My Casey's the opposite. Goes crazy with joy over any kind of wheelchair. When he sees one, he thinks he's about to get a treat. All because . . ." The elevator doors slid open. My fellow rider looked mystified. If he'd ever seen JP in action, he'd appreciate canine wheelchair obsession.

Casey and I were overdue to catch up with JP. I watched for him in all the usual places. The corner where we met, through snow and thaw and the greening of grass. The coffee shop he frequented. Every stretch of sidewalk wide enough for JP in his wheelchair to stop for a dog. How long had it been? A year at least. I hoped he hadn't fallen ill, then told myself not to overthink. How like me to fear the worst, when more likely he was living somewhere else, giving Milk-Bones to other dogs. Just because he used a wheelchair didn't mean he was sickly or frail. Perhaps he'd changed his schedule and would reappear any day.

We met other friendly people in wheelchairs. First up: a double amputee with the smile and complexion of Santa Claus. I'd seen him often, always alone, an orange caution flag on the back of his chair. When Casey pawed his lap (all laps look the same to him, with legs or without), I told him we'd been looking for the Milk-Bone man. "Maybe I should buy some dog treats," he said, after a meditative pause. I recognized that tone. It's the one I use myself for possibilities to file under "someday" (like a savory donut—irresistible, according to Yelp—from a café that closed for good while I was contemplating my first visit). JP would not be getting any competition from the man with the Santa Claus smile.

While waiting for a light to change, Casey and I stood beside a wheelchair user with rounded shoulders and a somber face. He didn't look like one to welcome Casey's best-pal routine. "Sorry, he thinks you have treats. I won't let him bother you."

"No worries. I love dogs. And I do have treats." The three of us shared a sweet moment, but he wasn't the Milk-Bone man.

Another day we found ourselves behind a huge electric wheelchair piloted by someone invisible except for a hot-pink topknot. Dog-walking had prompted me to learn some basic wheelchair manners; we'd have to pick our moment to pass. Casey and I take up a good chunk of the sidewalk. Then there are additional encroachments from construction hoardings, families with strollers and shambling students four abreast. As we scooted ahead, a call rang out from the chair: a tiny, bright-eyed young woman. I had to ask her to repeat what she was saying, which embarrassed only one of us. On the third or fourth try, I got it. "How old?"

When people ask Casey's age, they don't really care about the number. They want to meet him, and he's always in the mood. "May I pet him?" asked the woman. This time I understood her perfectly.

Casey had his paws all over the woman's shiny pink jacket, an exact match for her hair. She laughed when I told her about the Milk-Bone man. "Sorry, little man, I don't have any treats. But if I did, I'd give them to you."

As months went by with no sign of JP, I turned to my neighborhood's Facebook group. In my brief membership, I'd seen locals share tips on everything from the best street art to the juiciest banh mi sandwich. If you'd lost a cat or found a laptop, neighbors would pitch in to help. Casey and I had lost a person, but the group could surely help me find him. Did anyone have news of JP, the man on wheels with the bag of Milk-Bones?

"Now that you mention it," someone commented, "I haven't seen him in a long time, and I drive through the 'hood all day Monday through Friday."

Someone else thought he'd suffered "a couple of strokes" and would make inquiries. JP cured her dog's fear of anything with wheels, she said. Like Casey, the dog now thought every wheelchair was bringing him treats.

A couple of strokes. Talk about a close call. One stroke was bad enough.

The third commenter had visited JP last year. Our friend was in the hospital then, "not in good shape." He died not long afterward.

A collective sigh went up on Facebook. "His smile was so warming," one neighbor said. If she had a dog, she didn't say.

With JP gone, a little of Casey and me was gone too. That night I stumbled through my kitchen, set our plates on the table with a take-it-or-leave-it thud. I told Paul the only news of the day that mattered. "JP is dead."

When you choose a life partner, you are choosing the future witness to your grief. This never crossed my mind when I chose Paul. At 20, I couldn't imagine being impaled by grief. No one I loved had died; Paul became my first witness to loss after loss. Val, my mother, many friends and colleagues gone too soon. When my father died, just before Christmas, Paul heard me say, "Now he'll never call me drunk in the middle of the night." Then he saw me laid low by flu, with grief cascading from my nostrils and splitting my chest. What I wanted was not to be held but to be heard and seen as bereavement buffeted me.

My dead have all formed me, one way or another. They took with them pieces of my history that neither I nor anyone alive still remembered. JP knew nothing about me, except that I walked a cheerful dog named Casey. "Crazy puppy" to him and no one else. Our encounters on the street wouldn't add up to more than half an hour, yet I felt shockingly diminished by his passing. He saw me in unguarded moments, with faded lipstick and grass-stained shoes; I saw him spreading joy, a noble and necessary project. For all I know he once sold houses, designed gardens or fixed toilets, but doling out treats didn't matter any less. Happy dogs make people happy. I knew that; JP proved it. He died before I could ask if he played the piano. Before I could tell him, "I'm grateful that we met. I always look forward to seeing you." I liked to think that if time had allowed, I'd have opened a more searching conversation, but of course I was kidding myself. What I can get around to someday, I might not address today.

Paul had never met JP. We sat together listening to Casey snore. "I can't send even a note to his survivors. Nobody knows his last name." A pillar of the neighborhood doesn't need a name. It's all about the attitude, the fellow feeling—until grief shows up with nowhere to go but the pit of your stomach and the space behind your eyes. Every other place I'd lived, all the way back to Maynard Hall, I hardly knew my neighbors. JP was the first neighbor I had loved in the effortless sharing of delight. Before Casey, it seemed that I had enough love, but that was a defensive posture. No love, no mourning when it's over.

I woke the next day with JP on my mind. What had become of his cat? Or had I imagined the cat? Anyone who cared for animals as he did should have a furry creature in his lap. The espresso machine whirred; my spoon clinked against the cereal bowl. Casey's idea of the breakfast bell. He stood at my feet, eyes fixed on me with expectation. So he had stood in Liz's hallway when we met, and had every morning since then. In his world nothing had changed. We had places to go, but first there would be kibble.

The Dearest Freshness

A couple of lifetimes ago Val and I took a hike through the urban forest that winds through Toronto. I like to replay it in my mind. The memory jumps and crackles like an old home movie with missing scenes. Here we are mid-walk, following a creek bed where the footing gets rough. Now we crouch to make our way through tangled underbrush. We arrive at a meadow, big and bright, in some park I can't place anymore, farther from wherever we started than I thought we'd go. Sweat beads inside my sunhat. I'd like to bail; the subway can't be far away. Val chivvies me along with one more cheeky anecdote only she would tell, one more tenderly pointed insight into someone we know that only she would have. She's setting a pace, her muscled legs brown from other walks with other friends.

Into the frame saunters Casey, up to his usual antics— the tug, the jump, the shower of earth and dried leaves kicked up after peeing. Oh, Casey, you scamp. You're in the wrong decade, you never met Val and you haven't walked any part of this route.

Val and I met at the teen magazine, my first real job. She handed me a story in which the last page had been stitched together from scraps with turquoise yarn (Val recycled before it was trendy). I probably received the manuscript in my notion of office attire—cotton Mary Janes from China, a dirndl skirt from India and a faded T-shirt with no bra.

We were intimates through the silk-shirt years, the trading-up years, the births of children and the deaths of parents. My first book, her last. She remembered the fiction magazine I meant to start and then forgot. Yet she never knew who I became with a dog, which makes her seem more gone than ever.

They look good together on this trail, the fur on Casey's ears the same color as Val's tan. Val leads, he ambles here and there. So much sniffing to be done on this trail, so many trees in need of a spritz. I yell, "Hey, slow down!"

She smiles back at me, hands on hips, while Casey takes a good whiff of the teeming dirt. Whatever she's about to say will not be rushed. She keeps me waiting till we're almost face-to-face. Points to Casey, riffs on Gerard Manley Hopkins: "There lives the dearest foulness deep down things." Hopkins wrote, in praise of the natural world, "There lives the dearest freshness deep down things." If not for Val, who wove Hopkins into quite a few conversations, I wouldn't have discovered him. She had a homing instinct for the dearest freshness.

The first time I pictured the three of us out for a ramble, I'd just been overtaken by another wave of grief that came out of nowhere, less often than in the early days but with the same primal force. I could no sooner make an end of this than empty the oceans. Casey's presence in my daydream puzzled me. In 30 years of friendship, I couldn't recall Val showing any interest in dogs. Yet whatever compelled my attention was bound to hold hers, on a walk or over lunch at the Chinese dive with the surly waiters and the unsurpassed hot and sour soup. If I'd taken up mushroom farming, she'd have wanted all the details, then ransacked her store of arcane knowledge for some unlikely, irresistible connection between, say, mushrooms and *Six Feet Under*, the TV series that had us both hooked at the time of our one urban hike. So how could Val not be charmed by Casey and say something Val-ish about him?

When the brain tumor appeared, we were about to book our annual dinner in honor of both our birthdays, hers three days before mine. We always chose somewhere glamorous, never asked anyone else to share the fun. Until she died it didn't enter my mind that one of us would go before the other.

I tried to banish Casey from my daydream. He made me mourn what couldn't be instead of getting on with what could. I thought I should be grateful for the walk we had, not mourning the one that never happened. Casey was leading me into a thicket of regret and self-indulgence. Or so it seemed when he first bounded into the scene. Then I decided he belonged there, sniffing possibility under last season's fallen leaves. The dearest freshness was still out there, deep down things.

The Human Animal

Casey and I could walk to Corktown Common in about 20 minutes. Past a diner famous for specials unchanged since *Star Trek* was still on prime time ("Eat here, diet at home"), past the gaggle of wan smokers outside the *Globe and Mail* and the paler, thinner group huddled in the doorway of the methadone clinic. Into the heart of Corktown, where gabled Victorian rowhouses, once home to Irish immigrants, had been gussied up by professionals with money to spend on stained glass for their windows but no time for sipping coffee on the stoop. Casey could do his business in the middle of a pretty cul de sac, unobserved except by the terrorized cat taking shelter under a BMW.

Corktown Common owes its name to the local community, and its 18 acres to long-forgotten brownfields reimagined by the guru of park design, Michael Van Valkenburgh. The park had won an award from *Popular Science*, but where was everybody? Day after day, we had it mostly to ourselves. A park without visitors is like a book not yet opened by a reader, a garment not yet warmed by the skin of a wearer.

Alone or nearly so, we awakened Corktown Common with our senses, made it ours. For a human-canine pair, it offered particular advantages. Many loops, no traffic lights. No edible garbage to pry from Casey's mouth. Better yet, no squirrels to rile him. The trees were too young and sparse.

There are a few ways to enter Corktown Common, but I prefer to take the wooden footbridge over the marsh. As we cross I feel an inner release, like the lifting of a latch on an invisible gate. The bridge has no name except in my mind; I think of it as Blackbird Bridge, for all the red-wings that gather there in mating season. One morning I counted seven at once, likely well short of a record.

I never used to pay attention to birds, but at Corktown Common I kept an eye out for flickers of red against the sky. We must have come too close to a nest the day a red-wing tried to dive-bomb Casey, who didn't even bother to look up. The birds had been creating alarm among humans—attacks reported in the press, warnings posted along the waterfront. But Casey was born to chase birds, not to dodge them.

One high-summer morning we crossed the bridge to find a speckled frog in our path, still as a porcelain collectible. If Casey had shown any interest in the frog, I wouldn't have knelt to inspect it. But he didn't seem to realize it was alive. While he sniffed the air for more appealing prey, I took my time with the frog. His throat swelled with his breath. His back was every shade of green from army jacket to catwalk chartreuse. He took a single hop and planted himself in front of me, black eyes gleaming. I could have contemplated him for longer with no objection from Casey, but my knees told another story.

The two of us made our usual meandering circuit of the park, stopping at the places we like best. For Casey, a wide lawn dense with clover, the pee of other dogs and the occasional flattened remnants of small dead things on which he rolled to absorb the thrilling smell of their decay. For me, the staircase to a natural parapet, a lookout half-hidden by greenery. I could see out through the branches, but no one else could see in—not that there were many people to look. I could make out the bones of several rising condos yet hear leaves shake in a gust of air. "Good boy," I said, to remind Casey he wasn't forgotten and myself that I had an agreeable companion.

We worked our way back to Blackbird Bridge and found the frog exactly where we had left him, in a frog-size shadow, beneath a blade of grass that was a frog's equivalent of a tree tossed by a breeze. He'd found the perfect spot for a steamy morning in July and had no need to explore any further. His marsh and its rim were the known world.

High above the frog rose cattails in their summer glory, plump and iridescent. How had I reached my 60s without noticing how a cattail shimmers from certain sunny angles? Why had I never touched one? A fence stood between me and the cattails. To grasp the closest one, I had to strain. The spike felt rough yet trim, like the pelt of a well-fed animal. It has the most beautiful name, Google told me on the spot. Candlewick. And it's a flower, as dense with seeds as a patch of sky with stars. The frog would live out his days hopping distance from the marsh where cattails grew. For all he knew, cattails didn't exist.

The last time I looked—really looked—at a frog, I had a scalpel in my hand and a noseful of formaldehyde. As my biology teacher told it, we students had a few things in common with the rubbery corpses in our metal trays—all of us vertebrates, our vital organs similarly placed and performing similar functions. To know the inner workings of the frog was to know our own. *Oh, really? So what?*

Mr. Gambino strode among us with his pointer, which he stroked with a slow hand while deciding which of us to unnerve with a thwack on the desk and a question calculated to embarrass daydreamers like me. That day and every day, I deadpanned an answer that made no sense. He never got under my skin; it was always the other way around. Mr. Gambino would raise a thick, dark eyebrow and pause for effect. The whole class knew what he was about to say, with fresh exasperation: "*Miss* Maynard! You *amaze* me!"

What made me amazing was this: I refused to be amazed by life forms that had never gifted humankind with *The Odyssey*, the Brandenburg Concertos or some other monument to human artistry. I excelled at memorizing facts the night before an exam, but I tuned out the lesson biology has to impart about the interconnectedness of living things.

My intransigence had deep roots. Long before I confounded Mr. Gambino, I argued with my father when he said, cold sober and in a contemplative mood, "You know, Rona, people are animals."

I must have been about 11. My father had just looked up from his oatmeal and his book. Although I can't say for certain which book, I suspect it was Gavin Maxwell's bestselling memoir *Ring of Bright Water*, published in 1960 and a classic among tributes to the natural world. My father dove into that book and surfaced dripping with wonder. He told us all how Maxwell, a renegade aristocrat weary of human company, struck out for northern Scotland and made his home with a series of mischievous otters.

My father had been dead for more than 35 years when I finally read *Ring of Bright Water*. Now that I loved a dog and had found myself captivated by a frog, I could imagine loving otters, if only from a safe distance. I understood the bond between species; Casey had revealed it. I felt the truth of my father's statement, "People are animals," with my whole being instead of with my intellect.

A dog became a bond between the living and the dead. I could finally meet my father in Maxwell's wild landscape—to them unspoiled glory, to me unforgiving peril. I laughed out loud when Maxwell finds his home all but destroyed by an otter—books, trash, contents of drawers scattered every which way in a rampage so joyful it magnifies his love. My father must have read this passage to me, and I could hear it in his voice. When a book particularly delighted him, he couldn't keep it to himself.

Maxwell's otters appear well along in *Ring of Bright Water*, and rightly so. The book's true subject is what the otters meant to an ornery cuss in search of transcendence. Maxwell had starter relationships with a feral kitten, a ring-tailed lemur and a bush baby, but it was otters who became the true keepers of his heart. I felt the ache beneath the beauty of the prose, and knew my father must have felt it too. An ornery cuss himself, he too preferred other species to his own, showing more compassion for a starling family than he did to the rest of us Maynards. He once made a stab at filling the space in the eaves that contained their nest ("dirty birds," he said), but he acted too late. Stricken by the cheeping of the baby starlings and the frantic pecking of the mother, he ripped out his work. The starlings would live to terrorize the robins and befoul our steps.

At 11 I resented the book that moved my father. If ever a book could make me defy him out of sheer obstinacy, it was *Ring of Bright Water*. People couldn't possibly be animals, I claimed. We were more accomplished, more creative. *Better*. My father had no tolerance for sloppy thinking, but he didn't press his point. He must have sensed that this debate had nothing to do with biology. Accepting his failure to persuade me, he left the matter to my teachers.

And the teacher who opened my mind was a dog.

Fine Young Animals

There should have been a party for all our friends and family. Waitstaff pouring bubbly, glasses clinking, jazz trio in the background. A golden anniversary isn't just another day, but ours arrived seven months into the Covid-19 pandemic. Seven months of no social life. When we finally began to see friends, it was on park benches, six feet apart. We pondered the logistics of a Zoom celebration for scores of guests everywhere from Berlin to Shanghai, New York to Victoria, B.C. All those time zones made our heads spin, and for what? Tiny blurred faces on a screen. We'd keep it simple. Order steak dinner for two, work up an appetite on a family walk with Casey. Nothing to decide but the route. Paul left the choice to me.

Our day, October 20, happens to be my birthday. We were married on my twenty-first, the date on offer when I bought the license at city hall. We had lined up together for the license, giddy with resolve, but I had forgotten my ID and was sent home to fetch my birth certificate. One city hall lineup was enough for Paul, who had brought his own birth certificate and couldn't believe my fecklessness. In his mind, I had messed up. In my own, I had secured the best of omens. Had I come prepared the first time, we might have been offered October 19, a nothing date.

October 20 was a charmed date. Adult life had two gateways, the age of majority and marriage. On a single day, I'd enter both. It was 1970, a time of barefoot weddings in a field, with garlands instead of a veil and vows composed yourselves over wine or weed (then known as "dope"). That sounded like too much effort, and October seemed late for bare feet in the grass. We thought we'd slip into city hall between classes, trailed by a gaggle of friends. I counted on the wedding date, a Tuesday, to cast the glow we couldn't be bothered to cast ourselves. The marriage license cost ten dollars, a running joke between us ever since. "I paid five bucks for you." "Deal of a lifetime." Fifty years later, I knew exactly where we should honor that day—the campus where we met and the surrounding streets where we set about raising each other.

On an ordinary day Paul walks his hour with Casey and I walk mine, for no reason but convenience. The sight of us both lacing shoes by the door set Casey bouncing like mad. He knew this outing would be special, involving a ride somewhere with promising smells to check out. On October 20, 2020, a slightly overcast Tuesday afternoon, we might have been the only people in Toronto who drove to Ross Street for the sole purpose of starting a dog walk. The street has no park for the dog or extravagantly styled front doors to entertain the humans. On Ross neighbors don't compete to display the most artful jack-o'-lantern.

The one remarkable thing about Ross is how little it has changed since Paul lived there when we met. Students are still renting rooms, to judge from the abundance of well-used bikes on porches. Renovators have mostly left the street alone, despite its prime location directly south of the campus. All but a couple of its row houses still have chipped paint and overgrown front yards. They keep their counsel like rumpled old neighbors who ask for nothing but a few more years like the last quarter-century.

You can walk the entire length of Ross Street—all two blocks—and barely register its existence. Whoever owned Paul's former rooming house had painted it mauve in a stab at originality and dressed up the front porch with a brave geranium that overflowed its planter. If you didn't look closely, you'd miss the sagging roof of the porch. We looked. To us that house was a character, as worthy of attention as the face of an aged teacher who taught you what you weren't aware of learning. Someone in the household wheeled in and out on a ramp covered with utility matting. Had that person appeared, Casey might have jumped and bayed for joy (the continuing JP effect). As it was, none of us had any grounds for excitement. Said Paul with a sigh, "It's more rundown today than it was back then."

A white blind covered his old dormer window. The first time he took me to his room, I wondered how he could live in such spartan quarters. Anyone else would have had a brass water pipe and a Bob Dylan poster (Milton Glaser's with the psychedelic swirls of hair). Paul had only a tumble of paperbacks, heavy on P.G. Wodehouse, and two cardboard suitcases containing what passed for his wardrobe. "I can carry everything I own inside two suitcases," he said, as if worldly goods would turn him into a bourgeois fogey. I found this thrillingly odd. This Wodehouse fellow too. Who was he? Paul didn't seem to read Ken Kesey or Leonard Cohen.

He knew I'd taken a vow of chastity: no more sex without love. I'd declared myself in the coffee shop on our first date. The last suitor to hear this announcement regretfully took me at my word, unmanning himself in my eyes. Paul wasn't one to give up. As we stood naked under the bulb that dangled from the ceiling, he didn't tell me, "I know what you want" or "You have a great body." He said, looking us both up and down, "Fine young animals." I thought we could both stand to lose a few pounds, but he had enough confidence for two. His mattress lay under a sloping ceiling: We had to bow our heads before lying there. Something blew through me like wind in the timbers of an uninhabited house. Afterwards he said, "See what a difference love makes?"

I had always assumed love would sweep me off to a higher plane brushing the stars. This encounter anchored me to rumpled sheets the two of us had warmed. If I called it love, I might be setting myself up for disappointment. I might love Mr. Two Suitcases more than he loved me, and that I couldn't bear. And besides, I wasn't sure I dared love a man who had so little use for possessions.

For the longest time, I didn't have words for what had just happened between us. We didn't *make* love in a single coupling; we planted love like a tender seedling. It would reach toward the sun, wither from neglect, put out new shoots after pruning.

I took a photo of the guys in front of Paul's old digs on Ross. Casey pokes his nose through the chain-link fence. Whatever grows on the other side holds his interest without arousing his passion. To him there are no boring places for a sniff, only decent places and intoxicating ones. We couldn't offer rabbit sightings on the anniversary walk, but Casey waited while we composed shots in front of two more long-ago addresses.

The best thing about 30 Robert, the no-nonsense Victorian rowhouse of our newlywed days, used to be the adjacent convenience store where Anna sold me whatever I'd forgotten to buy up the street at Loblaws. She charged more, but I liked her too much to care. It was she who first winked at my belly and inquired, in an Eastern European accent, "Do I see right?" Paul and I had been talking of graduate school, but we literally fell into parenthood. Half-dressed for dinner with friends of my parents and already running late, we tumbled onto the madras bedspread purchased for my college dorm. We skipped the condom, thinking once wouldn't make any difference. Nine months later, we were fighting over who washed the dishes and why Paul got to sleep while I stayed up in the nursing chair. Anna must have heard us plummeting toward separation. If only I could tell her, "We made it. Fifty years today." An empty storefront marked the spot where she watched over me.

At 30 Sussex the bay window sparkled—a living room window when the house was new; for us a bedroom window sheltered by one of those deep Edwardian porches found in Toronto's more desirable neighborhoods. We lucked out with that apartment, our second-chance home after more than a year apart. On our first night back together, we fell asleep to the sound of Victoria Day fireworks. Bursts of light dappled the walls like a private celebration lavished on us from above; no blinds or curtains dimmed the radiance.

I thought our marriage was a riddle we had finally cracked. I didn't know that staying married means starting over time and again. We raised a child, sent that child into the world. Built two careers, closed our office doors for the last time. Acquired and got rid of all manner of stuff that once seemed essential—in the '70s a negative ionizer (what exactly did it do?), in the '90s a temperature-controlled wine room we eventually gave to the first taker with the skill to dismantle the thing and the truck to cart it away. I never understood why other people thought dogs were essential until Casey galloped into the space we had finally cleared of irrelevance.

University College, a neo-Romanesque fantasy, stirred memories for all three of us. In one of its ornately carved classrooms, Paul and I studied Jacobean drama. We felt no need for a second look. But as we passed the walkway to the Canine Cognition Lab, where no dogs had earned treats in some time, Casey tugged on the leash. He felt certain his friends were waiting, but the only people we met that day were young South Asian women in lavishly beaded gowns and coordinating hijabs. The steps of UC were the stage on which they swiveled this way and that for a photographer. They flanked a beauty with a slash of crimson in her veil and rhinestones encircling her forehead. A fairy tale would have said her lips were red as a rose, her eyes black as ebony. Paul asked, "Excuse me! Is this a bridal party?"

They laughed, a waterfall of amusement.

"Today is our 50th anniversary. We wish the bride a happy marriage."

"Amazing!" What amazed them was clear on their smooth and perfect faces—two geezers still tottering about with their dog, untroubled by their own decrepitude. When you've barely cracked your 20s, 50 years is older than your parents, older than you can conceive of being, ever. "Don't trust anyone over 30," we said in student days. Or, singing along with The Who, hoping to die before we got old. Fifty years before Paul and I took our vows, the Treaty of Versailles was new, Babe Ruth played his first season as a Yankee, and mystery readers discovered Hercule Poirot, of the pince-nez and patent leather shoes. Movie palaces drew crowds who didn't miss the voices of the stars; it was all about the faces then. Mary Pickford, Rudolph Valentino. Who remembered any of that? No one we wanted to know.

The sun was beginning to fade, and we had a party to start back home. Good caviar, delivered by a friend, chilling with a suitable champagne. A 1988 Lafite Rothschild in its basket, flowers from that shop that used to be the choice of society brides. We planned to dress up—for Paul a suit, for me the evening skirt and beaded top I once wore to galas. If Casey had the power and the capacity to choose the anniversary menu, we'd be ordering pizza (when he smells toasted dough, he knows he'll be getting Paul's crust). But steak it would be, and baked potatoes loaded to the hilt. Casey would take care of any stray bacon bits.

We didn't miss the jazz trio and the roomful of clinking glasses. Had our 50th come around some other year, we might have gone through the motions of throwing a bash. At 50 years you're expected to pull out the stops, but we're not party people. I'd have liked half a dozen loved faces at our table, which is just big enough for eight, I liked what we had even better.

If ever a day called for celebration, it was a Covid golden anniversary. "Celebrate" descends from the Latin "celebrare," a marriage of gladness and gravity. Its many meanings include festivities for a great occasion, but also the performance of a sacrament. It can refer to that pause in the hurly burly where we honor the noble or glorious. For seven months the world had paused. A woman I know had lost both her parents to the virus. A long-widowed friend missed her husband more than ever. Casey's walk led past tent cities and empty storefronts, while people swerved to avoid one another. Yet here I sat with Paul's hand on mine, our dog at our feet. The lilies flaring like vermilion wings as we drank the last of the claret, all three of us sated on the gifts of the day.

Epilogue

A celebration of life, if you're human, only happens after death. For a dog it happens every day, everywhere. The gladness of the quest for singular scents, the gravity of fixing each one in a brain designed for the task. Casey's busy snout is the canine song of praise for scat and pee, new grass and decaying leaves intermixed with who knows what.

I walk the seasons with Casey at Corktown Common, in a landscape that flowers and fades. An April rainfall brings out earthworms in Monet colors—many shades of violet, pink and coral culminating in the palest yellow. They strew the pavement, soon to be crushed underfoot. I bend to nudge one of them into the grass but my kindness misfires; the worm recoils.

A robin builds her nest in a redbud tree, one dried clump of duff at a time, nothing too small to be of use. Over a number of mornings, I observe her dedication to the task. I become so enthralled by this robin, my robin, that I share bird news with anyone who'll listen. *She's warming her eggs. The father's guarding the nest. The babies will hatch any day.* At last I arrive just in time to see a tiny head emerge, beak open wide, and my robin swoop down with a worm.

The raspberries turn plump and red enough to eat. Before Casey, I would nosh on a handful. Now I know that when a dog wants to pee, a raspberry bush will do as well as a hydrant. "I am a part of all that I have met," said Tennyson's Ulysses. So is Casey.

Early one morning we share the park with one other human, a woman in regal mid-life, with a high-heeled sandal in each hand. She wears a picture hat and a chiffon gown, the palest yellow, that sets off her black skin. Mother of the bride or second-chance bride? Either way, it's that time of year. She paces in a circle on the dewy grass, as if it were her private labyrinth. She doesn't see me watching her, sending good wishes on this fine Sunday for a wedding, the dandelions a splash of gold. Splendor in the grass, glory in the flower. Which Bible verse is that? I reach for my phone. Not the King James after all. Wordsworth, dear to my father.

In September the milkweed pods grow plump. Monarch butterflies alight on branches, too many to count. What to call a gathering of monarchs? "Roost," says Google. I prefer my own coinage, "festival."

Something here is always beginning. Come winter, it's the snowmen, rolled and packed and muffled in scarves. When Casey saw his first snowman, he reared up in squealing indignation. After that the snowman was just one more peeing spot. I watched it dwindle to a yellowed lump and the broken twigs that had once been arms. No snowman ever stirs him as the first one did. Passing lesser snowmen, I see it with my inward eye.

Any month of the year, I can pause beside Casey and let the moment envelop us. We are muddy grass between the pads of Casey's feet and in the treads of my hiking boots. We are the crackle of leaves, the crunch and glitter of snow. We are every intoxicating scent I'll never smell, and all the swirling colors that to him mean nothing at all. My song and his in wordless harmony.

We come home from a walk to find a condo neighbor in the elevator lobby. He's been watching Casey from afar and wants me to know what a great dog I have. "I've been a dog person all my life. Dogs make the most wonderful human beings." A maxim of his, if his smile is any indication.

"Yes, Casey is a wonderful dog." I hope I don't sound combative, but the distinction between canine and human animals is personal to me. With my senses awakened by a dog, I imagine our walks going on and on, wonder after wonder, to have and to hold. I can no sooner keep them than catch a shooting star, so I clear a space in the day to celebrate the brightest as they fly, a song of praise that won't end until I do. I've fallen that hard for this world.

Acknowledgments

When I started writing Facebook posts about the dog who had just won my heart, all I meant to do was have a little fun. I needed permission to take these cheerful stories more seriously. Kim Pittaway detected the makings of a book, and I could not be more grateful.

A book in search of its form is like a puppy tugging at the leash and spinning in all directions. Many people helped me guide *Starter Dog* into the world.

Marjorie Simmins, Robin Flicker and Pauline Couture read early pages and urged me to keep going.

Suzanne Boyd published my first crack at Casey's story in *Zoomer* Magazine.

Karen Levi-Lausa, whom I did not hire or know personally, generously critiqued the first draft and checked in months later to wish me well. Her email brought me hope as I struggled with a new draft.

Rebecca McClanahan's virtual workshop on memoir in essays revealed the answer to the last conundrum on my mind and made it seem obvious.

Every writer needs a perceptive final reader to bless the final draft. Joyce Kornblatt, whom I trust like a lifelong friend although our bond has been virtual and brief, did the honors from the Blue Mountains of Australia.

My sister in writing and life, Joyce Maynard, cheered me on at every juncture. Her judgment remains a touchstone. How lucky I am to have my own coach in the family.

My agent, Beverley Slopen, saw the promise of this book when it was still an unruly pup in need of training. We could not have found a better home than ECW Press: Susan Renouf, an editor's editor; Jen Knoch, a champion for the finest details of language; Jessica Albert, a designer who brought her love of dogs to the cover. Special thanks to our photographer, Heather Pollock, for capturing Casey's personality while he carried on like a scamp.

My husband, Paul Jones, had the wisdom to know we'd both be happier with a dog—and the good humor to keep me laughing as I wrote this book. Some of my favorite lines are really his. No Paul, no *Starter Dog*.

This book is also available as a Global Certified Accessible™ (GCA) ebook. ECW Press's ebooks are screen reader friendly and are built to meet the needs of those who are unable to read standard print due to blindness, low vision, dyslexia or a physical disability.

At ECW Press, we want you to enjoy our books in whatever format you like. If you've bought a print copy, just send an email to ebook@ecwpress.com and include:

- the book title
- the name of the store where you purchased it
- a screenshot or picture of your order/receipt number and your name
- your preference of file type: PDF (for desktop reading), ePub (for a phone/tablet, Kobo, or Nook), mobi (for Kindle)

A real person will respond to your email with your ebook attached. Please note this offer is only for copies bought for personal use and does not apply to school or library copies.

Thank you for supporting an independently owned Canadian publisher with your purchase!